Java-8: Test Your Aptitude

Chandrakant Naikodi, Suresh L & Badrinath G Srinivas

Java-8: Test Your Aptitude

Published by White Falcon Publishing
No. 335, Sector - 48 A
Chandigarh - 160047

ISBN - 978-1-943851-67-6

First Edition,
Copyright © 2016 Chandrakant Naikodi, Suresh L & Badrinath G Srinivas

ABOUT AUTHOR

- Dr Chandrakant Naikodi

  Dr. Chandrakant Naikodi is presently working as a Project Leader in MNC., Bangalore, India. He has received B.E. degree from the Visvesvaraya Technological University, Karnataka, India in 2004, and M.E. and Ph.D(CSE) degrees from Bangalore University, India in 2006 and 2014 respectively. His research interests include Computer Networks, MANETs, WSN, Programming Languages, Big Data and Databases. He has published many research papers in referred International Journals and Conferences. Also, he is the author of five technical books titled "C:Test Your Aptitude" and "1000 Questions and Answers in C++" published by Tata Mc-Graw Hill and other technical books titled "Programming in C and Data Structure", "Managing Big Data" and "Introduction to Computing and Problem Solving" by Vikas Publication which are widely used in both industry and academia. He has published over 50 papers in International Conferences and Journals.

- Dr. Suresh L

  Dr. Suresh L, Principal of CiTech, is ambitious and has been an eminent achiever throughout his service. He has over 24 years of teaching and administration experience. He is a source of inspiration for all the Cambrians, both faculties and students. He is a path setter for the development of both students and faculties. He is instrumental in conducting all college activities successfully. Apart from being a able leader, he is recognized as an eminent teacher. He is a member of Board of Studies / Examiners for various universities and autonomous Institutions. He has visited many countries like Singapore, Malaysia, Poland, Australia, UAE and Greece for academic pursuits. He gave Key Note address in the IEEE conference at Singapore. He is a Life member of ISTE and CSI and member of IEEE. He has published over 50 papers in National and International conferences and Journals. His current areas of interest include Data mining, Database Management Systems, Cloud Computing and Big Data. He had been a member of recruitment committees and resource person for many corporate companies.

- Dr. Badrinath G. Srinivas

  Dr Badrinath G. Srinivas is presently working as a Development Manager in Samsung India Electronics Pvt Ltd, India. He has received B.E. degree from the Visvesvaraya Technological University, Karnataka, India in 2003. He has received M.E. and Ph.D. degrees from Bangalore University, India in 2005 and Indian Institute of Technology Kanpur, India in 2012 respectively. His research interests include Biometrics, Pattern recognition, Computer Vision, Large Data Classification and Indexing for efficient searching, Human Computer Interface, Graphical and Gesture based authentication techniques robust to shoulder surfing and Wireless Networks. He has published many conference and journal articles in premium forums. He has also published four patents on authentication techniques robust shoulder security and human interface for audio files.

PREFACE

Java is object oriented programming language and is widely use for developing applications. From programmers point, it is robust, provides flexibility and vast. This book provides a comprehensive introduction to all the concepts of Java and also gives the differences between the concepts. Further for clarity and comfort of the reader, some tricky programming examples are provided and these examples covers concepts in considerable depth, yet makes their design and analysis accessible to all levels of readers. Examples are described such that it understood by anyone who has done little programming. But, depth of coverage or mathematical logic is not sacrificed.

This book concentrates on comparing basic language features, frequently asked questions and aptitude questions with syntax and examples wherever required. The text is intended to academic students, fresh graduates and professionals. For fresh graduates, it discusses Java concepts as well as subtle tricks of using the concepts. Further, this book gives learning in short time by highlighting all features of Java language. This book provides more than 200 examples which are compiled using Java-7/8. We have designed this book to be both versatile and complete.

For academic students, this textbook provides enjoyable introduction to the Java concepts. We have attempted to make every programming example interesting. To help academic students unfamiliar or difficult algorithms, we have attempted to describe each one in a step-by-step manner. We also provide careful explanations to understand the program.

For professionals, the wide range of examples for each concept the subtle tricks, makes it an excellent handbook. Most of the programming examples and differences that have been discussed have great practical utility. We therefore address implementation concerns and other engineering issues.

The authors will appreciate the suggestions or feedback from readers and users of this book. Kindly communicate your suggestions or comments through the following email addresses chandrakant.naikodi@{yahoo.in,gmail.com}.

Chandrakant Naikodi

Suresh L

Badrinath G. Srinivas

To Vaishnavi

Contents

Chapter 1

FAQs

Q   **What is Java?**

A   JAVA is a programming language and computing platform used to write utilities like games, business applications etc. It is targeted to allow the application developers "write once, run anywhere" (WORA). In other words, the code compiled on any platform does not need to be recompiled to run on another. Regardless of the Java applications are typically compiled to *bytecode* which can execute on any Java Virtual Machine (JVM) regardless of computer architecture.

Q   **Why Java?**

A   Java is a platform independent, fast, secure, reliable programming language. Java allows the application developers to "write once, run anywhere" (WORA).

Q   **Why Java is a called platform independent language?**

A   Java is a compiler and interpreter based language. In Java, *javac* command is used to compile the code which converts source code into byte code. Interpreter converts byte code into machine language code. After source code is compiled, it is converted to native code known as Byte-code which is portable and can be easily executed on all OSs as shown in Figure 1.1. Typically, Byte-code is represented in a hexa decimal format, so this format is unique on all platforms including Solaris, Windows or Linux. The interpreter reads the generated byte code out of compilation and translates it according to the current system.

Q   **What is a Byte-code in Java?**

A   Byte-code is the instruction set for JVM. Once compiled a Java program which generates Byte-code, it is run through a Java Virtual Machine(JVM). So Byte-code is the intermediate representation of program which is produced by the Java compiler by compiling that program code. This code is independent of machine and we can run on any machine's JVM. Byte-code acts as a machine code for JVM, but this machine code is platform specific whereas bytecode is platform independent. Byte-code is stored in .class file that is created after compiling the source code using Javac.

Q   **What is a ClassLoader in Java?**

A   A Java compiler converts a Java program into a .class file which is a collection of byte codes. Java class loader is responsible to load that class file from file system/network/any other location. Class loader again a another Java class, class loaders are three types : Bootstrap, Extension and System class loader.

1

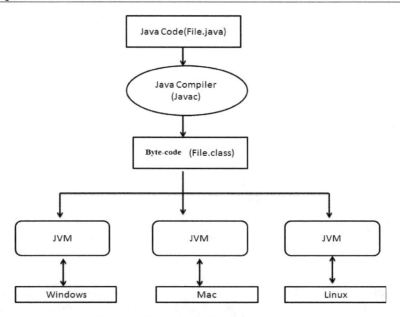

Figure 1.1 Java Code Execution Process

Q   **How should a minimal Java program looks like?**

A   Sample program:
```
class Test
{
public static void main(String arg[]) {
}
}
```
Here,
public => main() function can be called from anywhere.
static => main() does not belong to a specific object, it can be accessed without a instance.
void => main() returns no value.
main() => It is the name of a function. The main() is special function because it is the beginning point of the program.
String[] => It is an array of String.
args => It is the name of the String[], you can use any name.

Q   **What is a path?**

A   It is a location where the OS looks for executable files and commands.

Q   **What is a classpath?**

A   It is a parameter that provides the path where Java looks for loading class(s) or packages at run time and compile time.

Q   **What are the advantages (features) of Java?**

A   Advantages of Java are,

1. Platform independent (Multi-platform supporting language).

2. Object oriented language.

3. It is an open source programming language.

4. Supports garbage collection, hence memory management is automatic.

5. Used for dynamic web applications.

6. Used to create modular programs and reusable codes.

7. Robust and Secure.

8. Multithreaded.

Q   When you will get a java.lang.NullPointerException ?

A   Accessing a *NULL* Object or uninitialized Object.

Example:

```
String str=null;
if (str.equals("abc"))
{
    method ( );
}
```

Q   Why garbage collection is required?

A   Sometimes, some of the objects are not used anymore. However, these objects are holding the allocated resources. Thus, we need garbage collection to identify the resources allocated to such objects and be reclaimed and reused. If an object belonging to current running program and becomes unreachable, then that object is part of garbage collection. Further, garbage collection function will reduce the programmers burden for tracking the allocated memory.
Example: *System.gc();*
     You can explicitly reclaim the memory of a specific de-referenced object; to invoke the garbage collector requires a simple two-step process,
a). Create a Java *Runtime* object.
b). Invoke the *gc()* method

     Example:

```
Runtime g = Runtime.getRuntime ( );
g.gc ( );
```

Q   What is a *Class*?

A   Java class is a group of Java methods and variables. It acts as a blueprint or prototype or template from which *objects* are created. A class defines the state and behaviour of a real-world object. A class can extend only once but it can implement one or more interfaces. Rules of classes,

1. A class can have modifiers such as *public, protected* and *private*.

2. A class should have a name and same name is used for file name too.

3. The class body surrounded by braces i.e. {}.

4. The name of base class if any, preceded by the keyword *extends*. A class can only extend (subclass) one parent.

5. A class can implement more than one interface. A comma-separated list of interfaces implemented by the class, if any, preceded by the keyword *implements*.

Example:

```
public class A extends B implements C,D{// class
//Members like methods, constructors and variables
}
```

Q   What is an Object?

A   Objects are similar to real-world objects. Software objects are often used to model the real-world objects that you find in everyday life with state and behaviour.

Example:

```
public class Area {
   private int sqarea(int side){
     int area = side * side;
     return(area);
   }
   public static void main(String[] args){
         Area a = new Area ();    //Object creation
         System.out.println(a.sqarea(100));
   }
}
```

Output:
10000

Q   What is an *interface*?

A   An *interface* is the named collection of method definitions but without implementations (abstract methods). An *interface* can also include constant declarations. *Interface* methods are always instance methods. If you want to use them, there must be some associated object that implements the *interface*. You can not instantiate an interface directly, but you can instantiate a class that implements an *interface*.
Interface rules,

1. An *interface* can extend one of more interfaces but cannot extend class and cannot implement any interface.

2. You can declare *static constant* (final) variables inside interface.

3. All its methods in the *interface* are abstract methods implicitly, no *static* methods are allowed.

4. No *static* initialiser blocks are allowed inside the interface.

5. The *throws* clauses about exceptions in the interface's methods must exactly match the *throws* clauses of the implementing methods in the classes.

Example:

```
interface Inter1{
public void method1();
}
interface Inter2 extends Inter1{
public void method2();
public static final int val=100;
}
public class Test implements Inter2{
public void method1(){

System.out.println("Hello method1 !");

}
public void method2(){

System.out.println("Hello method2 !");

}
public static void main(String args[]){
Test test = new Test();
test.method1();
test.method2();

System.out.println("val= "+Inter2.val);

}
}
Output:
Hello method1 !
Hello method2 !
val= 100
```

Q   What is a synchronization?

A   Synchronization will come into picture when multithreading is used; synchronization is the capability to control the access of multiple threads working on shared resources. If multiple threads are accessing same variable, then they have to access it one by one.

Example:

```
public synchronized void method ()
{
// Body of method
}
```

Q   What is a Thread?

A   Thread is a program's execution path. It is an independent path of execution to take the advantage of multiple CPU available in a system. By having multiple threads you can speed up CPU bound task.

Q   What are different ways of using threads?

A   A thread can be implemented by using *Runnable* interface or by inheriting from the *Thread* class.

Example:

```
1)Implementing Runnable Interface:
import Java.lang.*;
public class ABCThread implements Runnable
{
        Thread T;
        public void run()
        {
        ....
        }
}


2)Extending Thread Class:
import Java.lang.*;
public class ABCThread extends Thread
{
        public void run()
        {
        ....
        }
}
```

Q   What is a Process?

A   It is an instance of a program running in a system. Typically, a process is a series of steps and decisions involved in the way task is completed.

Q   Is Java Pass-by-Reference Or Pass-by-Value?

A   Java supports Pass-by-Value and does not support Pass-by-Reference. In Pass-by-Value, a copy of the value to be passed, where as Pass-by-Reference means passing the address itself. Java passes objects as references and those references are passed by value. Further, Java primitives are also passed by value.

Example:

```
public class test {
        private String str="";
        test(String st){
        str=st;
        }

public String getstr() {
   return str;
        }

public void foo(test d) {
   d = new test("XYZ");
```

```
        System.out.println("foo:"+ d.getstr());
            }

public static void main(String str[]){
        test ABC = new test("TEST");
        System.out.println("Before foo-ABC :"+ ABC.getstr());
        ABC.foo(ABC);
        System.out.println("After foo -ABC :"+ ABC.getstr());
            }

}
```

OUTPUT:
Before foo-ABC :TEST
foo:XYZ
After foo -ABC :TEST

Q   **What is a *Map*?**

A   *Map* is an interface, which is used to map keys to values. A *Map* cannot contain duplicate keys, each key should map to at most one value. A *Map* is a part of *java.util* package. A *Map* permits *null* value.

Example:

```
import  Java.util.Map;
import  Java.util.Set;
import  Java.util.HashMap;
import  Java.util.Iterator;

public class MapTest{
    public static void main(String[] args) {
        Map<Object,String> intMap=new HashMap<Object, String>();
        // adding :Key->Value
        intMap.put(new Integer(108), "A");
        intMap.put(new Integer(78), "B");
        intMap.put(new Integer(98), "C");
                Set st=intMap.entrySet();
        Iterator valIt=st.iterator();

                while(valIt.hasNext()) {
        Map.Entry mp =(Map.Entry)valIt.next();
        int ky=(Integer)mp.getKey();
        String val=(String)mp.getValue();
        System.out.println("Key :"+ky+"  Value :"+val);
        }
    }
}
```

OUTPUT:
Key :78   Value :B
Key :108   Value :A
Key :98   Value :C

Q   **What is a *HashMap*?**

A   *Hashmap* is a class that implements *Map* extends AbstractMap class. Typically a *HashMap* contains values based on the key. A *HashMap* contains only unique elements and it may have one *null* key and multiple *null* values with no order.

Example:

```
import java.util.*;
class Test{
 public static void main(String args[]){
  HashMap<Integer,String> hm=new HashMap<Integer,String >();

  hm.put(1000,"Hari");
  hm.put(1001,"Rama");
  hm.put(1002,"Raghu");

  for(Map.Entry m:hm.entrySet()){
   System.out.println(m.getKey()+" "+m.getValue());
  }
 }
}
Output:
1002  Raghu
1000  Hari
1001  Rama
```

Q   **What is an *Iterator*?**

A   *java.util.Iterator* is an interface which allows you to walk through a collection of objects and operating on each object. Iterators contain a snapshot of the collection at the moment the *Iterator* was obtained. Thus, it is not advisable to modify the collection itself while traversing an iterator.
    The highlights are,

1. The *Iterator* interface is used to walk through the elements of a *Collection*.

2. Iterators let you process each element of a *Collection*.

3. Iterators are a generic way to go through all the elements of a *Collection* no matter how it is organized.

Example:

```
ArrayList<String> ABCList = new ArrayList<String >();
// Add Strings to ABCList
for (Iterator<String> it = ABCList.iterator(); it.hasNext(); ) {
    String str = it.next();
    System.out.println(str);
}
```

Q   **What is a abstract class?**

A   It is a class declared as *abstract*. It may or may not include abstract methods. Abstract classes cannot be instantiated, but they can be subclassed. Abstract method is declared without an implementation.

Example:

```
abstract class ABC        {
      public abstract void method();
      public static void methodABC()   {
   // code here
   }
}

class XYZ Extends ABC    {
      public method() {
      // code here
      }
}
```

Q   What is a *static* method?

A   When a method is declared as *static*, it can be accessed without creating an instance of the class and without referring to the object. Other important points are given below,

1. A *static* method belongs to a class as a whole and not to any one instance/object of that class. All *static* methods are implicitly *final*, because overriding is done based on the type of the object, and *static* methods are attached to a class not to an object.

2. A *static* method in a baseclass can be shadowed by another *static* method in a subclass, as long as the original method is not declared *final*. However, you can't override a *static* method with a non-static method.

3. A *static* method can only call other *static* methods.

4. A *static* method must only access *static* data.

5. A *static* method cannot reference to the current object using keywords *super* or *this*.

Example:

```
 public class MapTest    {
       public static void staticCall() {
    System.out.println("This is a static method");
       }

       public static void main(String[] args) {
       staticCall();
       }
}
```

Q   What is a *final* method?

A   A *final* keyword can be applied to methods, classes, data members, local variables and parameters depending on the context. A *final* class implicitly has all the methods as *final* but not necessarily the data members. A *final* class cannot be extended and *final* method cannot be overridden.

Example:

```java
public class ABC {
  public static final void foo() {
    System.out.println("foo()");
  }
}
```

Q   What are Checked and Unchecked Exception?

A   Checked exceptions will force you to catch the exception and handle to respond appropriately. These exceptions are important and business might require it. Checked exceptions extend from *Exception*. Methods should declare each checked exception it throws and caller to a method which throws a checked exception. Further method should either catch the exception or rethrow the exception itself.

Example:

```java
public class checkException extends Exception          {

}

public class ABC {
        static {
                    try {
                    method();
            } catch (InterruptedException e) {
                    throw new checkException();
            }
        }

        protected static void method() throws InterruptedException {
                    // method code
        }
}
```

Unchecked exceptions are *RuntimeException*, which extend from either *java.lang.RuntimeException* or *java.lang.Error*. These exceptions could be unexpected.

Example:

```java
public class runException extends RuntimeException {
    }

    public class ABC {
            static {
                try {
                method();
                } catch (InterruptedException e) {
                        throw new runException();
                }
            }

            protected static void method() throws InterruptedException {
                    // method code
            }
```

```
            }
```

Q   What is an Overriding?

A   Overriding is used in modifying the methods of the super class. In other words, a subclass method is overriding class of a superclass method. A subclass method will have same name, return type and arguments as a method in its superclass. When a method is invoked for an object of the class, it is the new definition of the method that is called and not the method definition from baseclass. Rules to override the methods,

1. The return type should be same.

2. Constructors cannot be overridden, but it can be overloaded like regular methods.

3. The argument list should be exactly the same as that of the overridden method.

4. *final* method cannot be overridden.

5. *static* method cannot be overridden, but can be re-declared.

6. Methods can be overridden only if they are inherited by the subclass.

7. The visibility cannot be more restrictive than the overridden method's access level.

8. Basically, if a method cannot be inherited then it cannot be overridden.

Example:

```java
class A {
   public void method() {
      System.out.println("A.method()");
   }
}

class B extends A       {
   public void method(){
      super.method();
      System.out.println("B.method()");
   }
}

public class ABC{
   public static void main(String args[]){
      A b = new B();
      b.method();
   }
}
```
Output:
A.method()
B.method()

Q   What is the default value of object declared as an instance variable?

A   The default value of object is *null*. When we create fields and array components, they are automatically

set to the following default values by the system:
numbers: 0 or 0.0
booleans: false
object references: null

Q What is serialization?

A Serialization is a mechanism or process of converting a set of object instances that contain references to each other into a linear stream of bytes which can then be transferred through a socket, stored to a file, or simply manipulated as a stream of data. This mechanism is used by RMI to pass objects between JVMs, either as arguments in a method invocation from a client to a server or as return values from a method invocation. If instances are to be serialized, then it has to implement an interface called *Serializable*, you pass the instance to the *ObjectOutputStream* which is connected to a *FileOutputStream*. It will save the object to a file. When you serialize an instance of a class, only non-static and non-transient instance data is saved, however Class definitions are not saved. Data will be available when you try to deserialize an object.
Example:

```
import java.io.*;
class Test {
public static void main(String args[]) {
// Object serialization
try {
SerClass object1 = new SerClass("Chandrakant", 33, 99.99);
System.out.println("object1: " + object1);
FileOutputStream fos = new FileOutputStream("ser");
ObjectOutputStream oos = new ObjectOutputStream(fos);
oos.writeObject(object1);
oos.flush();
oos.close();
}
catch(Exception e) {
System.out.println("Exception during serialization: " + e);
System.exit(0);
}
// Object deserialization
try {
SerClass object2;
FileInputStream fis = new FileInputStream("ser");
ObjectInputStream ois = new ObjectInputStream(fis);
object2 = (SerClass)ois.readObject();
ois.close();
System.out.println("object2: " + object2);
}
catch(Exception e) {
System.out.println("Exception during deserialization: " +
e);
System.exit(0);
}
}
```

```
}
class SerClass implements Serializable {
String str;
int age;
double total;
public SerClass(String str, int age, double total) {
this.str = str;
this.age = age;
this.total = total;
}
public String toString() {
return "str=" + str + "; age=" + age + "; total=" + total;
}
}
```

Output:
object1: str=Chandrakant; age=33; total=99.99
object2: str=Chandrakant; age=33; total=99.99

Q   What is Externalizable?

A   *Externalizable* is an interface that extends *Serializable* Interface. It sends data into streams in compressed format. *Externalizable* contains two methods *readExternal()* and *writeExternal()*. These methods will give you a control over the serialization mechanism and custom written mechanisms to perform the marshalling and unmarshalling functions. Thus if your class implements this interface, you can customize the serialization process by implementing those two methods.

Example:

```
class ABC extends XYZ implements Externalizable {
    public void writeExternal( ObjectOutput out )
    throws IOException {
        //Method code
    }
    public void readExternal( ObjectInput in )
     throws IOException, ClassNotFoundException {
        //Method code
    }
}
```

Q   What is overloading in Java?

A   Having more than one method with same name but different type of argument or different number of arguments available in same class or its subclass is called overloading. Return type and access specifier of method does not matter in method overloading.

Example:

```
class ABC{
    void add(int a,int b)        {   }
    void add (double a,double b)        {   }
    void add (float a, int b)   { }
}
```

Q   **What is a transient variable?**

A   The state of the variable will be always defaulted after the deserialisation. Hence transient instance fields are neither saved nor restored by the standard serialization mechanism.

Example: Let the current value of variable *ABC* is set to 9999. If it's default value was 0 when the object has been created. After deserialisation the variable *ABC* with current value 9999 will be defaulted to 0.

Q   **Where *serialization* is not applicable?**

A   In the following cases *serialization* is not applicable,

1. Transient Variable's state will be always defaulted.

2. Static Variables are not part of any particular state.

3. Super class fields are only handled if the super class itself is serializable.

Q   **What are wrapper classes?**

A   Java wrappers are classes that wrap up primitive values in classes or converts into object. This is required in most of the collection classes. Java provides specialized classes corresponding to each of the primitive data types such as, *Integer, Character, Double*, etc.

The wrapper classes also offer utility methods for converting to and from the *int/float/double/char* values they represent. All wrapper classes are *static*. So you can use them without creating an instance of the matching wrapper class. Further, once a wrapper has a value assigned to it, that value cannot be changed.

Example:

```java
import java.util.*;
 class ABC       {
    public static void main(String argv[])        {
        Vector vct = new Vector();
        vct.add(new Integer(100));
        vct.add(new Integer(200));

    for(int i=0; i < vct.size();i ++)    {
        Integer in =(Integer) vct.get(i);
        System.out.println(in.intValue());
    }
    }
}
Output:
100
200
```

Q   **What are the different ways to handle exceptions?**

A   Two ways to handle exceptions,

1. Basic Try-Catch-Finally: Put desired code in a *try* block followed by a *catch* block to catch the exceptions. The *finally* block always executes when the *try* block exits irrespective of unexpected exception. Example:

```
public void Divide(){
        try {
         int res = div(200,0);
         System.out.println(res);
        } catch (BadNumberException ex) {
            System.out.println(ex.getMessage());
        }
        finally {
        System.out.println("Done !");
        }
    }
public void div(int Divide, int DivideBy)
    throws BadNumberException{
        if(DivideBy == 0){
            throw new BadNumberException("Cannot divide by Zero");
        }
        return Divide/DivideBy;
    }
```

2. Exception Hierarchies: Several exception classes inherit directly from *Exception* class. The caller of the method to handle exceptions should invoke desired exceptions from the hierarchy in the throw's clause.

Example:

```
public void method() throws IOException, FileNotFoundException{
//code
}
```

Q   What are executions criteria of *finally* block?

A   If a *try* block is executed, then after its completion *finally* block will automatically executes. If you write *return* as the last statement in the *try* block, the *finally* block will still execute. After *finally* block execution only, *return* statement is executed. However, *finally* block will not execute if *System.exit(0);* is executed. In other words, after executing the *System.exit(0);* the control immediately goes out of the program, and thus *finally* never executes.

Example:

```
try{
        //some code
    } catch(Exception ex){
        //some code
    } finally {
        //some code
    }
```

Q   What is finalize() ?

A   The *finalize* method will be executed before the object is garbage collected. Each class inherits the *finalize()* method from *java.lang.Object*, which is invoked by the garbage collector when it determines no more references exists to the object. Also, the *finalize()* method is never invoked more than once for any object. The *Object* class *finalize* method may be overridden by any class.

Example:

```
protected void finalize() throws Throwable {
    try {
        // resource closing
    } finally {
        super.finalize();
    }
}
```

If any exception thrown by *finalize()* during garbage collection, it halts the finalization. Finalize can be used to release the resources like closing the file, etc.

Q   What is Locale class?

A   *java.util.Locale* object represents a specific geographical, political or cultural region.

Example:

```
Locale[] locs = Locale.getAvailableLocales();
    for(int j = 0; j < locs.length; j++){
        String lang = locs[j].getLanguage();
        String count = locs[j].getCountry();
        String locName = locs[j].getDisplayName();
        System.out.println(j + ": " + lang + ", "
        + count + ", " + locName);
    }
```

Q   What is a daemon thread?

A   A daemon thread is a low priority service provider which runs intermittently in the back ground during runtime for garbage collection operation.
setDaemon(boolean) : This method is used to set the thread as daemon or not.
isDaemon() : This method is used to check weather the thread is daemon or not.

Example:

```
public class DaemThread extends Thread {}
public static void main(String[] args) {
 DaemThread thrd = new DaemThread();
 thrd.setDaemon(true);
 thrd.start();
}
```

Q   What is JDBC (Java Database Connectivity) connection? How to achieve a JDBC connection?

A   The JDBC is a Java API which defines interfaces and classes for reading/writing database applications in Java by making database connections. Steps to get Data Base connection,

1. Register the database driver: e.g. *Class.forName(specific DB driver class);*

2. Create a database connection:
    e.g.*Connection conn = DriverManager.getConnection(url,username,password);*

3. Create a query: e.g. *PreparedStatement stm= Conn.prepareStatement(SQL query);*

4. Execute the query: e.g. *stm.exceuteUpdate();*

Q   **What method all threads must implement?**

A   The *run()* method should be implemented in all threads, despite it is a subclass of *Thread* or *Runnable* interface.

Example: Extending *Thread* class.

```
class ABCThread extends Thread {
    public ABCThread (String str) {
        super(str);
    }
    public void run() {
            try {
                //code
            } catch (InterruptedException e) {
                }
    }
}
```

Example:Implementing *Runnable* interface.

```
class ABCRun implements Runnable{
char ch;
ABCRun(char c) {
    ch = c;
}
public void run() {
        try {
            //code
        } catch( InterruptedException e ) {
            }
            }
}
```

Q   **What modifiers are allowed for methods and variables in an interface?**

A   Modifiers allowed for variables in Interface are *public, static* and *final*.
Modifiers allowed for methods in Interface are *public* and *abstract* .

Example:

```
public interface ABC {
    public static final int val = 1;
    public abstract void mehtod(...);
}
```

Q   **What are types of modifier?**

A   Access modifiers are used to set the visibility and accessibility of a class, its member variables and methods.

Control Modifiers	Applicable	Description
public	class	Accessible anywhere or visible to all classes everywhere.
public	interface	Accessible anywhere or visible to all classes everywhere.
public	member	Accessible where ever its class is visible.
private	member	Visible to the class only.
protected	member	Visible to the package and all its subclasses.
abstract	class	Cannot be instantiated and this class contains unimplemented methods.
abstract	interface	By default, all interfaces are abstract. Optional in declarations.
abstract	method	Methods without body is its signature. The enclosing class is always abstract.
static	class	An inner class becomes top-level class.
static	method	Class's methods are invoked using the class name with dot operator.
static	field	Class's fields are invoked through using the name of class.
static	initializer	It is executed when the class is loaded, rather than when an instance is created.
final	class	Cannot be subclassed.
final	method	Methods cannot be overridden and dynamically looked up.
final	field	Fields cannot change its value and these are compile- time constants.
final	variable	Cannot change variable's value.
synchronized	method	Synchronized keyword is used preferably for methods where multithreading is implemented. For a static method, a lock is acquired for the class before executing the method. For a non-static method, a lock is acquired for the specific object instance.
transient	field	Cannot serialize with the object.
volatile	field	Accessed by unsynchronized threads.
native	method	Methods with no body are its signature and platform-dependent.
none (package) or default modifier	class	Accessible only within package.
none (package) or default modifier	interface	Accessible only within package.

none(package) or default modifier	member	Accessible only within package.
strictfp	class	In this class, all methods are implicitly strictfp.
strictfp	method	All floating-point operations done are strictly conforms to the IEEE 754 standard. All values should be expressed as IEEE float or double values.

Q **What is a variable?**

A A variable is used to hold the data and that can be modified during execution of the program. Each variable has a specific type, which tells the size and layout of the variable's memory; the values range that can be stored within that memory; and the operations set that can be applied to the variable. In Java, all variables must be declared before they can be used.

The syntax of variable declaration: *data-type variable [= value][, variable [= value] ...] ;* Here, data type is valid Java's datatypes and variable is the name of the variable.

Example:

int a, b, c; // Declaring three ints, a, b, and c.

int a = 100, b = 100;

Q **What is a scope of variable?**

A Scope of a variable means the access range of the variable inside the code. The scope of variable refers to the accessibility of a variable. Variables defined inside a block are only accessible from within the block, i.e, the variable scope is the block in which it is defined. There are many ways we can declare variables in different places:

1. Class fields in a class body called class-level variables.

2. Variables as parameters of a method or constructor.

3. Variables in a method's body or a constructor's body.

4. Variable within a statement block, like inside a *while, do-while* or *for* block.

Example:

```
public class ABC {
  public static void main(String[] args) {
    int outerBlk = 100;

    {
      int innerBlk = 200;
      System.out.println("innerBlk = " + innerBlk);
      System.out.println("outerBlk = " + outerBlk);
    }
```

```
        int innerBlk = 300;
        System.out.println("innerBlk = " + innerBlk);
        System.out.println("outerBlk = " + outerBlk);
    }
}
Output:
outerBlk = 100
innerBlk = 300
outerBlk = 100
```

Q   **What are the different types of variable scopes?**

A   The scope of a variable is determined by the place and context in which the variable is declared. Types of Scopes,

   1. Local variable: These variables are defined within a method. They remain accessible only during the course of execution of the method. When the method completes its execution, these variables fall out of the scope.

   2. Instance variable: Typically these are object level variables. They are initialized to default values at the time of object creation and remain accessible as long as the object is existing/reachable.

   3. Static variable: These variables are called class level variables because they are not tied to any particular object instance. They are initialized for the first time when the class is loaded into JVM and remain as long as the class is reloaded.

Q   **What is the default value of the local variables?**

A   There is no defined default value for local variable created. Also for primitives nor object references there is no defined default value. You need to specify the value of variable explicitly, otherwise Java compiler will not compile the code.

Q   **What is the scope of variable?**

A   The block of code within which the variable is accessible defines the scope of a variable.
The scope determines,
a. When variable is created?
b. When it possibly becomes a candidate for destruction?

Q   **What are primitive variable types?**

A   Please refer below table, few data types are system dependent.

Data Type	Bit Size	Usage	Signed	Range of Values
boolean	1	true or false	No	True or false
char	16	Unicode character	No	0 to $2^{16} - 1$
byte	8	Very small integer number	Yes	-2^7 to $2^7 - 1$

short	16	Small integer number	Yes	-2^{15} to $2^{15} - 1$
int	32	Integer number	Yes	-2^{31} to $2^{31} - 1$
long	64	Large integer number	Yes	-2^{63} to $2^{63} - 1$
float	32	Single precision decimal number	Yes	$+3.4e^{38}$ to $+1.4e^{-45}$
double	64	Double precision decimal number	Yes	$+1.8e^{308}$ to $+4.9e^{-324}$

Q   **What are Control flow statements?**

A   Control flow statements changes the flow of execution. Generally control flow performed using decision-making, looping and branching. In other words, control flow statement decides whether certain lines of code should be executed or not. However, the decision is made based on the state of the program. Control flow gives flexibility to conditionally execute particular blocks of the code.

The below table shows the categories of control flow statements.

Category	Keyword	Purpose
Selection or Decision-Making Statements	*if, if-else and switch*	Execute a block or set of statements only if certain conditions/cases are met.
Loop Statements	*while, do-while and for*	This allows you to execute the set of statements repeatedly or looped through a fixed number of times or condition is satisfied.
Exception	*throw, throws, try-catch and finally*	Exception statements are normally used to handle unusual events or errors that arises while a program is running.
Branch Statements	*continue, break and return*	The *continue* statements are used in looping statements to force another iteration of the loop before reaching the end of the current one. The *break* statements are used in looping/switch to come out immediately from the loop or to end a switch case. The *return* statements are used to force return from method. The *return* can also used to pass values back to the calling method.

Q   **What is expression and when it is required?**

A   An expression is a combination of variables, constants, operators and method invocations which are evaluated to a single value. Expressions can have a single operation or multiple operations combined to form a compound expression. Expression is required in below scenarios,

1. To compute the values,
   Example : 45 + 35 * 98 − 34;

2. To assign values to the variables,
   Example:

   ```
   int a = 88, b = 99;
   int exp = a * b;
   ```

3. To control the flow of execution,
   Example:

   ```
   int a = 55, b = 68;

   if ( a * b > 300)
   {
   // statements
   }
   ```

Expressions are the basic components of statements and these statements are terminated by the semicolon character ';'.

Q   Explain the working of Java Virtual Machine (JVM) in Java?

A   JVM is a software that is responsible for running Java programs (runtime environment). JVM interprets the *bytecode* (.class file which contains virtual machine instructions) to a machine dependent native code. The output of JVM (the native code) contains low-level instructions which are executable by the processors which process the native code.

JVM contains the following components:

1. Class loader: Dynamically loads Java classes into the JVM.

2. Bytecode checker: Verifies bytecode, which make sure like type checking, "edge" of a method and so on.

3. JIT compiler and interpreter: A JIT Compiler translates byte code into machine code and then execute the machine code. Whereas, interpreters converts bytecode into machine dependent code.

Q   What is a package?

A   It is a mechanism of organizing Java classes into namespaces. Java packages can be stored in JAR files (compressed files), allowing classes to download faster as a group rather than one at a time. Packages typically used to organize classes belonging to the same category or providing similar functionality and also provide a unique namespace for the types it contains. Classes in the same package can access each other's members depending upon the visibility.

Example:

```
package animals;
import behavior.*;
public class man {
  public static void main(String[] args) {
      // statments
  }
}
```

Q What is singleton class?

A   Only one object can be created at a time from a class called singleton class. This class contains a static method that returns its instance. A new singleton instance will be created when a singleton class is garbage-collected or reloaded.

Example:

```
    public class ABCSingleton {
            private static ABCSingleton inst = null;
            protected ABCSingleton() {
            }
  public static ABCSingleton getinst() {
    if(inst == null) {
       inst = new ABCSingleton();
    }
    return inst;
  }
}
```

Q List the disadvantages of Threads in Java.

A

1. There could be a race condition, end up in deadlock issue and starvation may happen.

2. Threads are totally Operating Systems dependent.

3. Global variables are shared between threads, hence there are chances of getting unexpected data.

4. Threads are executed serially (looks like parallel execution but actually it is serial execution) may increase the time complexity.

5. Many library functions are not thread safe. They are not a safe to have them in the control flow.

6. The whole application crashes if any one of the threads crashes.

7. Unlike processes, memory crash in one thread kills other threads because of sharing the same memory.

Q What is a referent?

A   A *final* keyword is used in the declaration of reference variables or constants. These referent variable value is immutable and cannot be modified to refer to any other object. Thus the *final* specifier applies to the value of the variable itself and not to the object referenced by the variable.

Example: *private final String Str = Hi;*

Q   **Does Java support multiple inheritance?**

A   Multiple inheritance in Java is not directly achievable, but indirectly it can be done through implementing number of interfaces. In Java, you can extend only one class by other class. However, multiple inheritance causes more problems and confusion than it solves.

Example:

```java
import java.lang.*;
import java.io.*;
interface Inter
{
        void getPerc();
}
class Test
{
        String name;
        int roll_no,mark1,mark2;
        Test(String n, int r, int m1, int m2)
        {
                name=n;
                roll_no=r;
                mark1=m1;
                mark2=m2;
        }
        void Show()
        {
                System.out.println ("Name of Test: "+name);
                System.out.println ("Roll No. of Test: "+roll_no);
                System.out.println ("Marks of Kannada: "+mark1);
                System.out.println ("Marks of English: "+mark2);
        }
}
class Res extends Test implements Inter
{
        Res(String n, int r, int m1, int m2)
        {
                super(n,r,m1,m2);
        }
        public void getPerc()
        {
                int total=(mark1+mark2);
                float percent=total*100/200;
                System.out.println ("Percentage: "+percent+"%");
        }
        void Show()
        {
                super.Show();
        }
}
class Main
```

```
{
        public static void main(String args[])
        {
                Res R = new Res("Chandrakant",1001,98,97);
                R.Show();
                R.getPerc();
        }
}
```
Output:
Name of Test: Chandrakant
Roll No. of Test: 1001
Marks of Kannada 1: 98
Marks of English 2: 97
Percentage: 97.0%

Q   **What is a *List* interface?**

A   *List* interface is a part of *java.util* package. *List* can implement *Vector* and *ArrayList* class. *List* value can get by *Iterator* interface. It is ordered collection of objects. *List* interface can add *value* elements using *add* (value) method with *value* as argument and remove a element using *remove(index)* method with *index* as the argument. There are other operations available too, please refer Java doc.

Example:

```
import Java.util.List;
import Java.util.ArrayList;
import Java.util.Iterator;
public class listTest {
    public static void main(String[] args) {
        List<String> lst = new ArrayList<String>();
        lst.add("value 1");
        lst.add("value 2");
        lst.add("value 3");
        Iterator iter=lst.iterator();

        while(iter.hasNext())   {
          String val=(String)iter.next();
          System.out.println(val);
        }
    }
}
```
output:
value 1
value 2
value 3

Q   **Can we enforce garbage collection in Java?**

A   No, you cannot force garbage collection. But you can request or hint JVM explicitly for garbage collection by calling the method *System.gc()*. However, it is not guaranteed to start immediately. The *System.gc()* is a low priority thread of JVM.

Q   How can you call a constructor from another constructor and super class?

A   By using *this*() and *super*() respectively.

Example:

```java
public class Test1 {
    public Test1() {
        this("Test1");   // this function
    }
    public Test1(String arg) {
        System.out.println(arg);
    }
public static void main(String[] args) {
                new Test1();
                }
}
public class Test2 extends Test1{
    public Test2() {
        super();           // super function
    }
    public Test2(String arg) {
        System.out.println(arg);
    }

    public static void main(String[] args) {
                new Test2();
                }
}
output:
Test1
```

Q   What is de-serialization?

A   It is the process of restoring the state of an object. Deserialization is the inverse process of serialization, reconstructing an object from a byte stream to the same state in which the object was previously serialized.

Example:

```java
ObjectInputStream desObj = new ObjectInputStream(new
FileInputStream(new File(text.txt)));
System.out.println("The content : "+ desObj.readObject());
desObj.close();
```

Q   What is a native method?

A   It is a method implemented using language (typically C or C++) other than Java. The Java native method is a way to merge the solutions developed using C or C++ programming into Java.

Q   Which is the base class for all classes in Java?

A   *The java.lang.Object* is the base class for all classes including arrays. It is the root of the class hierarchy, hence every class has *Object* as a superclass.

Q   **What is casting? How many types of casting?**

A   It is the process of converting one type into another or changing an entity of one data type into another. There are two types of casting.

1. Primitive type casting: To convert larger data types to smaller data types.

   Example: Convert from boolean to byte

   ```java
   boolean bl = true;
   byte bt = 1;
   bt = (byte)(bl?1:0);
   ```

2. Object references casting: It is used to refer to an object by a compatible class or interface or array type reference. With objects, you can cast an instance of a subclass to its parent class and known as up casting. Down casting is to cast from a base class to a more specific class. The cast does not convert the object, rather it just asserts it.

   Example:

   ```java
   class Animal {
           int a = 123;
   }
   class Mammal extends Animal { }
   class Cat extends Mammal { }
   class Dog extends Mammal { }

   public class TestUpcast {
   public static void main(String[] args) {
           Cat cat = new Cat();
       System.out.println(cat.a);
       Mammal mam = cat; // upcasting here !
       System.out.println(mam.a);
           }
   }
   Output:
   123
   123
   ```

Q   **What is a hashCode?**

A   It is a number (32-bit signed int) that allows an object to be managed by a hash-based data structure. A *hashcode* is treated as equivalent to an object for fast computation using all or most of the internal state of an object. It uses all or most of the space of 32-bit integers in a fairly uniform way and likely to be different even for objects that are very similar. If you are overriding *hashCode* you need to override *equals* method also.

   Example:

   ```java
   public class Test{
           public static void main(String[] args){
                   String str1=new String("Java");
                   String str2=new String("KAVA");
   ```

```
            String str3=new String("Java");
            System.out.print("str1 == str3:" + str1 == str3);
            System.out.println(str1.equals(str3));
            System.out.println(str1.hashCode());
            System.out.println(str3.hashCode());
            System.out.println("str1 == str2:"+str1 == str2);
            System.out.println(str1.equals(str2));
            System.out.println(str1.hashCode());
            System.out.println(str2.hashCode());
        }
}
```

Output: false true
2269730
2269730
false
false
2269730
2299521

Q   **What is a class loader in Java?**

A   Class loader is one of the Java class and it is responsible for loading the business classes. All JVM contains one class loader called primordial class loader. When a class is loaded, all of its associated references are also loaded. The process of loading happens recursively until all classes needed are loaded. However, it is not necessarily loads all classes of the application. Unreferenced classes are not loaded until the time they are referenced.

The steps followed by a class loader:

1. Check weather class was already loaded.

2. If not loaded, ask base class loader to load the class.

3. If base class loader cannot load a class, attempt to load it in *this* class loader.

Example:

```
public class Test {
        public static void main(String [] args) {
        try {
                Class clz = Class.forName("Java.util.HashSet");
                if (clz != null) {
                Object obj = clz.newInstance();
                ((Java.util.HashSet)obj).add("ONE");
                ((Java.util.HashSet)obj).add("TWO");
                Java.util.Iterator it =
                ((Java.util.HashSet)obj).iterator();
                while (it.hasNext()){
                        System.out.println(it.next() );
                }
                }
        } catch (Exception e) {
                System.err.println("Problem in loadind a class " +
```

```
                  "Java.util.HashSet");
                  }
          }
}
output:
TWO
ONE
```

Q   What is JAR (Java archive) file?

A   This is a file format that enables you to bundle multiple files into a single archive file. JAR files will contain a file named MANIFEST.MF inside the folder named META-INF, and it has the version and other features information of jar file.

Q   What is JIT (Just In Time compiler)?

A   It compiles Java bytecode into native code or platform specific executable code that is immediately executed. JIT compiler option should be used especially if the method is repeatedly reused in the code. The JIT compiler maintains a table called the V-table, it has two sub-tables one for the addresses of the bytecode and another for the native code that is created using the bytecode. During the first time execution of a method, it converts the bytecode into the native code by the JIT compiler and address of the native code of method is stored in the address table. Then during subsequent execution of the method, previously created native code is invoked for execution. Thus it improves the speed of the execution.

Q   What is a internationalization?

A   Internationalization is the process of designing an application, so that it can be applicable to various languages and regions without modifications.

Q   What is a volatile variable?

A   Volatile is used to indicate that a variable's value will be modified by different threads.
The value of this variable will never be cached in the thread locally. All reads and writes corresponding to volatile variable will be updated in its main memory location. Access to the variable acts as though it is enclosed in a synchronized block, synchronized on it.

Example:

```
/**
 * A SingletonClass Instance is declared as volatile
 * variable to ensure every thread see updated value
 * for singInsta.
 */
public class SingletonClass{
private static volatile SingletonClass singInsta;
public static SingletonClass getInstance(){
   if(singInsta == null){
           synchronized(SingletonClass.class){
             if(singInsta == null)
               singInsta = new SingletonClass();
           }
```

```
                }
    return singInsta;
}
}
```

Q   **What is a abstraction?**

A   An abstraction is a concept in Java, that is used to show only the essential features and hide certain details of the object.

Example:

```
public class Main{
        public static void main(String args[]){
        A a = new B();
        a.method();
    }
}
abstract class A {
    public abstract void method();
}
class B extends A{
        public void method(){
                System.out.println("method...");
        }
}
```

Q   **What is a encapsulation?**

A   Encapsulation describes the ability of an object to hide its data and methods from the rest of the world. This technique involves making the fields in a class private (it cannot be accessed by anyone outside the class) and providing access to the fields via public methods. This process also known as data hiding. Access to the data and code is tightly controlled by an interface.

The main advantage of encapsulation is the ability to modify our implemented code without breaking the code of others who use our code. With this feature encapsulation gives maintainability, flexibility and extensibility to our code.

Example:

```
public class Test        {
        private String name;
        public void setName(String nm){
                name = nm;
        }

        public String getName(){
                return name;
        }

        public static void main(String args[]){
                Test t = new Test();
                t.setName("Chandru");
```

```
                         System.out.print("Name:  " + t.getName());
          }
}
```
Output:
Name: Chandru

Q   What is a inheritance?

A   Inheritance is the ability to create new classes based on existing classes or capability of a class to use the properties and methods of another class while adding its own functionality. It is useful to reuse the existing code. This defines *is-a* relationship between a superclass and its subclasses.
Inheritance is not possible in below cases,

1. A subclass can extend only one super class at a time.

2. Private members of the super class are not inherited by the subclass and can only be indirectly accessed by the setters and getters of public methods.

3. Since constructors and initializer blocks are not members of a class, they are not inherited by a subclass.

4. Members that have default accessibility in the superclass are also not inherited by subclasses in other packages, further, these members are only accessible by their simple names in subclasses within the same package as the superclass.

Q   How state and behaviour is associated to objects?

A   OOPs objects are conceptually similar to real-time objects which consist of state and related behaviour expressed through the members of class. In real programming, an object stores its state in fields and its behaviour in the methods.
Example: A bird can have state like name and its behaviour like flying.

Q   What is a Socket? What are advantages and disadvantages?

A   A socket is a link between two programs running on the network to achieve two-way communication. Socket classes are used to represent the connection between a client program and a server program. The *java.net* package has following two classes,
Socket: To implement the client side of the connection.
ServerSocket: To implement the server side of the connection.
Further, following are some of the advantages of Java sockets:

1. Sockets are flexible and sufficient.

2. Efficient for general communications.

3. Sockets cause low network traffic.

Disadvantages of Java Sockets:

1. Security restrictions.

2. Socket based communications allows only to send packets of raw data between applications.

Q   List the primitive types and the corresponding wrapper classes.

A   Wrapper classes are defined in *java.lang* package. Primitive types and its respective wrapper class are as follows,

Primitive Type	Wrapper Class
boolean	Boolean
char	Character
byte	Byte
short	Short
int	Integer
long	Long
float	Float
double	Double
void	Void

Q   Does a class inherit the constructors of its base (super) class?

A   A class does not inherit constructors from any of its base class. A constructor cannot be inherited, since in subclasses it has a different name. See below example,

```
class A {
    A();
}
class B extends A{
    B();
}
```

Here, since constructor of class A creates an object of type A and constructor of class B creates an object of class B. But, you can still use constructors from A inside B's implementation.

Q   What is the use of *System* class?

A   *System* class is used to provide access to system resources. *System* class cannot be instantiated. The uses of *System* class includes, standard output, error output streams, to copy a portion of an array, standard input and access to externally defined properties and environment variables.

Q   When explicit object casting is needed? Give example of the same.

A   You need to do explicit casting when you assign a super class object to a variable of a subclass's data type.

Example: Vehicle is super class and Car is subclass.

```
Vehicle v;
Car c;
c = (Car) v;
```

Q   What is the order of catch statements for super class and subclass?

A   Exception of subclasses has to be caught first.

Q   What is Object class in Java?

A   The *Object* class is a superclass for all user-defined Java classes and Java's class libraries. A Java object is an instance of any class which is derived from the *Object* class. Usually, when a class is defined in Java, implicitly the object class is inherited.
   Example:

```
public class ABC {}
```

is same as

```
public class ABC extends Object{}
```

Q   If some important event has happened in one class, how to inform this action to other class?

A   If you are using regular classes, use the observer interface to update the event in the other class. If these classes implements/extends *Runnable/Thread* classes, then use *notify()* or *notifyAll()*.

Q   What are the different levels of locking by using synchronization?

A   Different levels of locking,

1. Block level lock.
   Example: synchronized (this) { //code }

2. Method level lock.
   Example: public synchronized void method() { //code }

3. Object level lock.
   Example:
   ```
   private Object lock = new Object();
   synchronized(lock) {
               //code
   }
   ```

4. Class level lock
   Example:
   ```
   class Test {
      static synchronized public method() {
         //code
      }
   }
   ```

Q   What is the use of prepared statement in Java?

A   *PreparedStatement* is derived from more general class statement. *PreparedStatement*s are precompiled statements. They are generally used in bulk processing of data to speed up the process of inserting, updating and deleting.

   Example:

```
Class.forName("com.mysql.jdbc.Driver");
Connection con = DriverManager.getConnection("jdbc:mysql://
localhost:3306/jdbctutorial","root","root");
PreparedStatement prest =
con.prepareStatement("UPDATE EMPLOYEES SET SALARY = 10000");
ResultSet rs = prest.executeQuery();
```

Q   What is callable statement?

A   It is used to invoke the stored procedures. You can obtain the *callablestatement* from connection using the following methods.
prepareCall(String sql)
prepareCall(String sql, int resultSetType, int resultSetConcurrency)

Q   What is annotations in Java?

A   Annotations in Java are used to add the meta-data facility to Java elements. It is the data about a program that is not part of the program and has no impact on the operation of the code. Annotations can be applied to program declarations of classes, fields, methods and other program elements.
    Annotations used as,

1. Information for the compiler: The compiler those detect errors or suppress warnings can use Annotations.

2. Compile-time processing: Software tools can process annotation information to generate code, etc.

3. Deployment-time processing: Software tools can process annotation information to generate XML files, etc.

4. Runtime processing: Annotations are available at runtime.

Example:

```
@Tree (
    Name = "Mango",
    Age = "23"
)
class ABC()
```

Q   What is Autoboxing?

A   Autoboxing is a new feature in Java 5. Java compiler makes automatic conversion between the primitive (basic) types and their corresponding object of wrapper classes (eg, *int* to *Integer*, *double* to *Double*, etc).

    Example:

```
int  num=10;
Intager numObj = num; // this is allowed in Java 5 and onwards.
```

Q   What is Auto-unboxing?

A   Auto-unboxing is a way to automatically convert the wrapper types into their primitive equivalents for assignments or method or constructor invocations.

Example:

```
int num = 0;
num = new Integer(10); // this is allowed in Java 5 and onwards.
```

Q   Why we should prefer primitive data types rather than object wrapper classes?

A   Primitive data types are faster than the corresponding wrapper types and immune (can't be changed after creation) compared to wrapper types.

Q   What are scanners?

A   The *java.util.Scanner* is a new feature of Java 5, it is used to read values from *System.in* or a file. A simple text scanner which can parse primitive types and strings using regular expressions. Basically, a *Scanner* breaks its input value into tokens using a delimiter pattern(by default matches whitespace). The resulting tokens may then be converted into values of different types using the various next (*nextInt*, *nextLong*, etc) methods.

Example:

```
Scanner scan = new Scanner(System.in);
int num = scan.nextInt();
```

Q   What is *instanceof* operator?

A   It is a type comparison operator. Determines if an object belongs to a specific class or implements a specific interface. It returns *true* if an object is an instance of the class or if the object implements the interface, otherwise it returns *false*.

Example:

```
public class Test {
public static void main(String[] args){
  String str1 = "abc";
  String str2 = null;
  if(str1 instanceof java.lang.String)
        System.out.println("str1:It is a String object !");
  else
        System.out.println("str1:It is not a String object !");
  if(str2 instanceof java.lang.String)
        System.out.println("str2:It is a String object !");
  else
        System.out.println("str2:It is not a String object !");
        }
}
Output:
str1:It is a String object !
str2:It is not a String object !
```

Q   What is a literal?

A   A literal is the representation of a fixed/physical value. Literals are represented directly in the code without requiring computation.

Example:

```
char c = 'C';
boolean bl = false;
int i = 3;
byte bt = 2;
```

Q   **How to copy arrays ?**

A   In Java, *System* class has an *arraycopy* method (library method) that can be used to copy the elements from one array into another efficiently.
Method:
public static void arraycopy(Object source, int source_ position,Object destination, int destination_ position, int length)
Here,
Object source: specifies the source array name.
Object destination: specifies the destination array name.
int source_ position: starting position in the source array.
int destination_ position: starting position in the destination array.
int length :the number of array elements to copy
Example:

```
    public static void main(String[] args) {
        char[] src = { '1', '2', '3', '4', '5', '6', '7' };
        char[] dest = new char[10];
        System.out.println("Before copy:"+new String(dest));
        System.arraycopy(src, 3, dest, 0, 3);
        System.out.println("After copy:"+new String(dest));
    }
}
Output:
Before copy:
After copy:456
```

Q   **What are branching statements available in Java?**

A   Branching statements are *break, continue* and *return*. The *break* statement is used to break the loop or *switch* statement. The *continue* statement skips the current iteration of a *for, while* or *do-while* loop. The *return* is used to explicitly return from a method.

Q   **What are nested classes?**

A   It is the process of defining a class within another class. Nested class is a member of its enclosing class. Nested is a logical grouping of classes that are only used in one place, and provides more readability and maintainable code with encapsulation. There are two types of nested classes classified into (i) static nested classes and (ii) non static nested classes (inner classes).

(i) Static nested classes: It is associated with its outer class and cannot refer directly to instance variables or methods defined in its enclosing class. It can use them only through an object reference.

Example:

```
class Outer {
        class Inner      {
                public   void innerMethod() {
                        System.out.println("innerMethod");
                }
        }

        public   void outerMethod() {
                System.out.println("outerMethod");
        }
}

public class Test {
        public static void main(String[] args) {
                Outer outobj=new Outer();
                Outer.Inner innerobj=outobj.new  Inner();
                outobj.outerMethod();
                innerobj.innerMethod();
        }
}
```
Output:
outerMethod
innerMethod

(ii) Non static nested classes (inner classes): Inner class is associated with an instance of its enclosing class and has direct access to that object's methods and fields. Further, it cannot define any static members itself.

Example:

```
class Outer {
        static   class Inner {
        public   void innerMethod() {
        System.out.println("innerMethod");
        }
}

        public   void outerMethod() {
                System.out.println("outerMethod");
        }
}

public class Test {
        public static void main(String[] args) {
        Outer outobj=new Outer();
        Outer.Inner innerobj=new Outer.Inner();
        outobj.outerMethod();
        innerobj.innerMethod();
        }
}
```
Output:
outerMethod
innerMethod

Rules:

a) You cannot create a static member inside the nested class.

b) Nested class can be declared abstract or final.

c) If you have a static nested class, you cannot access the methods and variables of the outer class from the static nested inner class.

d) To have instance of nested class, it is necessary to have an instance of outer class.

Q   **What is *Enum* Type?**

A   Fields of *Enum* consist of a fixed set of constants. The instance of *Enum* describes values, where the set of possible values are finite. Enumerated type is used when the most important information is the existence of the value. All enums implicitly extend *java.lang.Enum*.

Example:

```
enum Day {
SUNDAY, MONDAY, TUESDAY, WEDNESDAY,THURSDAY, FRIDAY, SATURDAY
}
public class Test {
        public static void main(String args[])  {
                Day d = Day.THURSDAY;

                switch(d) {
                case SUNDAY:
                        System.out.println("Day-7");
                        break;
                case MONDAY:
                        System.out.println("Day-1");
                        break;
                case TUESDAY:
                        System.out.println("Day-2");
                        break;
                case WEDNESDAY:
                        System.out.println("Day-3");
                        break;
                case THURSDAY:
                        System.out.println("Day-4");
                        break;
                case FRIDAY:
                        System.out.println("Day-5");
                        break;
                case SATURDAY:
                        System.out.println("Day-6");
                        break;
                default:
                        System.out.println("Invalid day !");

                }
        }
}
Output:
Day-4
```

Q   **What are the methods inherited from *Object* superclass?**

A   Every class inherits the instance methods of *Object*. Listed few of methods inherited from *Object*,

1. *protected object clone() throws CloneNotSupportedException*
   Creates and returns a copy of this object.

2. *public boolean equals(Object Chk)*
   Indicates whether any other object is "equal to" the argument object *Chk*.

3. *protected void finalize() throws Throwable*
   Garbage collector invokes this on an object, if garbage collector determines that there are no more references to the object.

4. *public final Class getClass()*
   Runtime class of an object is returned.

5. *public int hashCode()*
   Hash code value for the object is returned.

6. *public String toString()*
   String representation of the object is returned.

7. public final void notify()
   Invokes the first thread that called *wait()* on object.

8. *public final void notifyAll()*
   Invokes all the threads that called *wait()* on object. However, threads are executed based on priority.

9. *public final void wait()*
   Causes current thread to wait until another thread invokes the *notify()* method or the *notifyAll()* method for this object.

10. *public final void wait(long $time_out$)*
    Causes current thread to wait until any another thread invokes *notify(all)* method or *notifyAll()* method for current object or after a specified amount of time has elapsed.

11. *public final void wait(long $time_out$, int $nano_s$)*
    Contemporary thread to wait until another thread invokes the *notify()* method or the *notifyAll()* method for this object, or some other thread interrupts the present thread, or a certain amount of real time has gone.

Q   **What is bounded type parameters?**

A   It is a parameter of type with one or more bounds. The bounds restrict the set of types that can be used as type arguments and give access to the methods defined by the bounds.

Example:

```
public class Test {
        public static <S extends Comparable<S>> S max(S a, S b, S c) {
                S max = a;
                if ( b.compareTo( max ) > 0 ){
                        max = b;
                }
```

```
            if ( c.compareTo( max ) > 0 ){
                    max = c;
            }

            return max;
    }
    public static void main( String args[] )            {
            System.out.println( "max is:"+max( 11, 22, 1 ) );
            System.out.println( "max is:"+max( 1.1, 2.2, 0.5 ) );
            System.out.println( "max is:"+max( "B", "A", "D" ) );

    }
}
```
Output:
max is:22
max is:2.2
max is :D

Q   **What is a Constructor?**

A   Constructors are similar to methods but it has same name as objects. During creation of a new instance (a new object) of a class using the *new* keyword, a constructor for that class is called. Rules of constructors are,

1. Constructors are used to initialize the instance variables of an object.

2. Default constructor is created only if there are no constructors. They do not have return types.

3. The first line of a constructor must either be a call on another constructor in the same class (this), or a call on the superclass constructor (using super).

4. Constructor cannot be inherited.

Example:

```
public class Test          {
        private int v;
        public Test(){
                System.out.println("Hi");
        }
        public Test(int val){
                v=val;
        }

        public static void main( String args[] )            {
                Test t= new Test();
                Test t1= new Test(100);
                System.out.println(t1.v);

        }
}
```
Output:Hi
100

Q   What are types of object creation techniques in Java?

A   We can create objects in the following ways,

1. By using *new* keyword:

   Example:

   ```
   Test obj = new Test();
   ```

2. By using *Class.forName()*:

   Example:

   ```
   Test obj = (Test) Class.forName( com.abc.Test ).newInstance();
   ```

3. By using *clone()*:

   Example:

   ```
   Test obj= new Test(); Test obj1= obj.clone();
   ```

4. By using object deserialization technique

   Example:

   ```
   ObjectInputStream obj =
   new ObjectInputStream(inputStream );
   Test obj1 = (Test) obj.readObject();
   ```

5. By using class loader:

   Example:

   ```
   this.getClass().getClassLoader().
   loadClass( com.abc.Test ).newInstance();
   ```

Q   What is a *final* modifier?

A   The *final* modifier keyword does not allow the value to be modified.
a) *final* Classes: *final* class cannot be sub classed.
b) *final* Variables: *final* variable cannot be altered once it is initialized.
c) *final* Methods: *final* method cannot be overridden by subclasses.

Q   What is the use of *static* block?

A   Static block will be executed exactly once when the class is first loaded into JVM. Before accessing the main method, the static block will be executed.

Example:

```
public class Test          {
       static{
                // statements or Code
       }
}
```

Q **What is the *Set* interface?**

A The *Set* interface provides methods for accessing the elements of a finite mathematical set without duplicate elements. It contains all methods which are implementations of the *List* interface which includes,
i. *HashSet*
ii. *TreeSet*
iii.*LinkedHashSet*
iv. *EnumSet*

Q **What is a *HashSet* ?**

A a) A *HashSet* is an unsorted and unordered set.
b) It uses the *hashcode* of the object being inserted.
c) Duplicates are not allowed.

Example:

```
import Java.util.*;
public class Test {
        public static void main(String [] args) {
                int size;
                HashSet <String>hSet = new HashSet <String >();
                String str1 = "A", str2 = "Z";
                Iterator iterator;
                hSet.add(str1);
                hSet.add(str2);
                System.out.print("Values : ");
                iterator = hSet.iterator();

                while (iterator.hasNext()){
                        System.out.print(iterator.next() + " ");
                }
        }
}
Output: Values: Z A
```

Q **What is a *TreeSet* ?**

A *TreeSet* keeps the elements in sorted order. The elements are sorted according to the usual order of elements or by the comparator provided at creation time.

Example:

```
import Java.util.*;
public class Test{
        public static void main(String[] args) {
                TreeSet <Integer>tree = new TreeSet<Integer >();
                tree.add(123);
                tree.add(345);
                tree.add(12);
```

```
                        System.out.print("Tree before deletion: ");
                        Iterator iterator;
                        iterator = tree.iterator();
                        while (iterator.hasNext()){
                                System.out.println(iterator.next() );
                        }
                        System.out.println("");
                        if (tree.remove(12)){
                                System.out.println("12 is deleted");
                        }
                        else{
                                System.out.println("12 doesn't exist!");
                        }
                        System.out.print("Tree after deletion: ");
                        iterator = tree.iterator();
                        while (iterator.hasNext()){
                                System.out.println(iterator.next() );
                        }
                }
        }
}
Output: Tree before deletion: 12
123
345
12 is deleted
Tree after deletion: 123
345
```

Q   What is a *Map*?

A   A *Map* stores pairs of key and value with associations between *keys* and *values*. However, it has some rules, some of them are listed below,

1. Both *keys* and *values* are objects.

2. Using *key*, you can find its value.

3. The *keys* must be unique, but the *values* may be duplicated.

4. *Map*s can accept a *null* key and *null* values.

5. For inserting, deleting and locating elements in a *Map*, the *HashMap* offers the best performance.

Some of the implementations of the *List* interface are
i. *HashMap*
ii. *HashTable*
iii.*TreeMap*
iv. *EnumMap*

Q   What is the *Comparable* interface?

A   This method compares two objects (*Object1* and *Object2*) and returns a integer, the return value is positive if first object *Object1* is greater than *Object2*, return value is zero if both objects *Object1* and

Object2 are equal. If return value is negative then *Object1* is less than *Object2*. The objects of the class which are required to be ordered should implementing this *Comparable* interface. The *Comparable* interface is used to sort collections and array of objects using the *Collections.sort()* and *java.utils.Arrays.sort()* methods respectively. All classes implementing the *Comparable* interface must implement the *compareTo()* method that has the return type as an integer. The generic format of *Comparable* interface is,

```
interface Comparable<S> \newline
```

where S is the name of the type parameter.

Example:

```
import Java.util.Comparator;
public class Test implements Comparator{
        public int compare(Object valS, Object valT){
                String NameS = ( (Test1) valS ).getName();
                String NameT = ( (Test1) valT ).getName();
                return NameS.compareTo(NameT);
        }
}
```

Q   What is a *TreeMap* ?

A   In a *TreeMap*, the data will be sorted in non-decreasing order of key's class or by the comparator provided at creation time. *TreeMap* is based on the Red-Black tree data structure. *TreeMap* implements the *SortedMap* interface which extends the *Map* interface. *TreeMap* is your better solution when you need to traverse the keys in a sorted order.

Example:

```
import Java.util.*;
class Test {
        public static void main(String args[]) {
                TreeMap tMap = new TreeMap();
                tMap.put("Vinod", new Double(22));
                tMap.put("Shankar", new Double(44));
                tMap.put("Kiran", new Double(11));
                tMap.put("Chandru", new Double(1));
                Set set = tMap.entrySet();
                Iterator i = set.iterator();
                while(i.hasNext()) {
                        Map.Entry map = (Map.Entry)i.next();
                        System.out.print(map.getKey() + ": ");
                        System.out.println(map.getValue());
                }
        }
}
Output:
Chandru: 1.0
Kiran: 11.0
Shankar: 44.0
Vinod: 22.0
```

Q   What is a Default constructor?

A   It is a constructor which is automatically created by the compiler without parameters (default). The default constructor calls the default base (parent) constructor (*super()*) and initializes all instance variables to default value (*zero/null/false* for numeric types, object references and booleans respectively). This constructor does not perform any actions or initializations.

Example:

```
Test  t = new  Test  ();
```

Q   Why is the Java *main*() method *static*?

A   The JVM interpreter will call the program's public *main()* method to start the program without creating an instance of the class (because it is static), and the program does not return data to the JVM interpreter when it ends. The *main()* method is part of its class and not part of the objects.

Q   When can an object reference be cast to an *interface* reference?

A   An object reference is cast to an interface reference as soon as the object implements the referenced interface.

Q   Which class do all other classes extend by default?

A   *Object* class.

Q   Does Java support multi-level inheritance or multiple inheritances?

A   Java supports multi-level inheritance. In the below example we have three classes; Car, Honda and HondaVXMT. The class Honda extends Car and class HondaVXMT extends Honda. With the help of this Multilevel hierarchy setup our HondaVXMT class is able to use the methods of both the classes (Car and Honda).

```java
class Car{
        public Car()
        {
                System.out.println("Class Car");
        }
        public void vehicleType()
        {
                System.out.println("Vehicle Type: Car");
        }
}
class Honda extends Car{
        public Honda()
        {
                System.out.println("Class Honda");
        }
        public void brand()
        {
                System.out.println("Brand: Honda");
```

```
        }
        public void speed()
        {
                System.out.println("Max: 120Kmph");
        }
}
public class HondaVXMT extends Honda{

        public HondaVXMT()
        {
                System.out.println("Honda Model: VXMT");
        }
        public void speed()
                {
                        System.out.println("Max: 100Kmph");
                }
        public static void main(String args[])
        {
                HondaVXMT obj=new HondaVXMT();
                obj.vehicleType();
                obj.brand();
                obj.speed();
        }
}
```
Output:
Class Car
Class Honda
Honda Model: VXMT
Vehicle Type: Car
Brand: Honda
Max: 100Kmph

Q   What is MVC Architecture?

A   MVC stands for Model View Controller. Model can include bean and EJB. View can include Html, JSP and Controller, and can also include *Servlet*. MVC pattern or architecture is a sequence of action interactions starting with view, then controller and then to model based on the data persistence. Model is responsible for holding the application state, view for displaying the current model and controller handles the event.

Q   What is runtime polymorphism?

A   Polymorphism allows you to define one interface and have multiple implementations e.g., method overriding. A method in subclass overrides the method in its super classes with the same name and signature. Runtime polymorphism is also called as dynamic method dispatch. At runtime, which version of the method will be invoked is based on the type of actual object stored in that reference variable and not on the type of the reference variable.

Example:

```
class T {
  void method() {
```

```
      System.out.println("I am a T.");
    }
}
class T1 extends T {
  void method() {
    System.out.println("I am a T1.");
  }
}
class T2 extends T {
  void method() {
    System.out.println("I am a T2.");
  }
}
class T3 extends T {
  void method() {
    System.out.println("I am a T3.");
  }
}

class Test {
  public static void main(String[] args) {
    T ref1 = new T();
    T ref2 = new T1();
    T ref3 = new T2();
    T ref4 = new T3();
    ref1.method();
    ref2.method();
    ref3.method();
    ref4.method();
  }
}
Output:
I am a T.
I am a T1.
I am a T2.
I am a T3.
```

Q   **What is property (.*properties*) file in Java?**

A   The .*properties* is an extension of files to store the configurable parameters of an application hence they are called as property resource bundles. They can also be used for storing strings for internationalization and localization. Each line in a .*properties* file normally stores a single property and each parameter in properties file is stored as a pair of strings, one is storing key (name of the parameter), and the other is storing the value. Some example for formats:

a) key = value

b) key: value

c) key value

or ! is used to denote a comment in properties file and the backwards slash is used to escape a character.

Example: Content of *TestProperty.properties* file:

Test = This is a Test

Test1 = This is a Test1

The content of Test.Java file:

```
import Java.io.FileNotFoundException;
import Java.io.FileReader;
import Java.io.IOException;
import Java.util.Properties;

public class Test {
        public static void main(String[] args) {
                Test test = new Test();
                test.readProperties();
        }

public void readProperties(){
        FileReader filerdr = null;
        try     {
                Properties prps = new Properties();
                filerdr =
                new FileReader("C:\\TestProperty.properties");
                prps.load(filerdr);
                System.out.println("Properties: " + prps.toString());
        }catch(FileNotFoundException exe){
                exe.printStackTrace();
        }catch(IOException ioe){
                ioe.printStackTrace();
        }finally{
                try{
                        filerdr.close();
                }catch(IOException e){
                        e.printStackTrace();
                }
        }
        }
}
```

```
Output:
Properties: {Test1=This is a Test1, Test=This is a Test}
```

Q   What is a reflection?

A   It is used to inspect and dynamically call classes, methods, attributes, etc. at runtime. Assume, you have an object of an unknown type in Java and you would like to call a *getValue* method on it. If the called method exists (you can confirm if interface existed) verified using reflection, your code can look at the object and find out if it has a method called *getValue*, and then call it if you required to call.

Example:

```
Test test = HelloObj.getClass().getTest("getValue", null);
test.invoke(HelloObj, null);
```

Q   How to execute PL-SQL in Java?

A   Calling a PL/SQL function from a JDBC application involves following steps,

1) Write a PL-SQL statements in a *String*.

2) Create and prepare a JDBC *CallableStatement*(similar to the *PreparedStatement*) object that contains a call to your PL/SQL function.

3) Register the output parameter for your PL/SQL function.

4) Provide all of the required parameter values to your PL/SQL function.

5) Call the *execute*() method for your *CallableStatement* object, which then performs the call to your PL/SQL procedure.

6) Read the returned value from your PL/SQL function.

Example:

```
public   static int count(Connection conn) {
        int count=0;
    // query
        StringBuffer plSQL = new StringBuffer ();
        plSQL.append("CREATE OR REPLACE FUNCTION counting
        RETURN number is  " +
        "Name varchar (200);  " +
        "cnt NUMBER :=  0;    "  +
        "CURSOR Cursor IS     SELECT name from TABLE ;  " +
    "BEGIN "+
    "OPEN Cursor;  " +
    "LOOP  " +
     " FETCH Cursor INTO Name;  " +
      "EXIT WHEN Cursor%NOTFOUND;     " +
      "cnt :=  cnt +1;  " +
    "END LOOP;  " +
    "CLOSE Cursor;  " +
    "return(cnt );  " +
    "END;"  );
      Java.sql.Statement st=null ;
      CallableStatement cs=null ;
      try {
      st=conn.createStatement ();
      st.execute(plSQL.toString ());
      cs=conn.prepareCall("{?=call  versionValidation }");
      cs.registerOutParameter (1 ,Types.INTEGER);
      cs.execute ();
      count= cs.getInt (1);
      }catch(Exception exe ){
              try {
              exe.printStackTrace ();
              st.close ();
              cs.close ();
              }catch(Exception e){}
              return count ;
      }
        return count ;
```

}

Q   **What happens when you invoke a thread's interrupt method while it is sleeping or waiting?**

A   In this case task enters into the ready state.

Q   **What is the purpose of the *File* class?**

A   The object of *File* class is used to access the files and directories of a local file system.

Q   **How to read attributes/columns of database tables through JDBC(Java)?**

A   Select COLUMN_NAME from USER_TAB_COLUMNS where TABLE_NAME = 'TABLE_NAME' order by column_id; This query will list out all column names existed in the TABLE_NAME. USER_TAB_COLUMNS is having many attributes like DATA_TYPE, DATA_LENGTH, NULLABLE etc.

Q   **What is a JDBC connection pool?**

A   JDBC connection pool is nothing but the method of storing established connections in the memory or pool. JDBC connection pool is important when your application is tasked with servicing many concurrent users within the requirements of sub-second response time. Once that particular database task is completed, the connection is returned back to the pool. Every time a database connection needs to be established, a request is made to pool or any object which holds all the connections to provide a connection.

Q   **What happens when a thread cannot acquire a lock on an object?**

A   It enters to the waiting state until the lock becomes available.

Q   **Can an unreachable object become reachable again?**

A   Yes. It can happen when the object's *finalize()* method is invoked and the object performs an process which causes it to become accessible to reachable objects.

Q   **What classes of exceptions may be caught by a catch clause?**

A   It can catch any exception that may be assigned to the *Throwable* type including *Error* and *Exception* types.

Q   **What happens if an exception is not caught in a program?**

A   An uncaught exception will invoke *uncaughtException()* method of the thread's *ThreadGroup*, which eventually results in the killing of program from which it is thrown.

Q   **Which arithmetic operations can result in the throwing of an *ArithmeticException*?**

A   / and %

Q   **What is the use of a statement block?**

A   A statement block is used to organize a succession of statements as a solitary statement group.

Q   **Can you call one constructor from another if a class has multiple constructors?**

A   Yes, this is possible by using *this()*.

Example:

```
public class Test {
        int x = 10;
        Test (){
                this (2);
        }
        Test(int x){
                this.x=x;
        }

        public static void main(String args[])  {
                Test t=new Test ();
                System.out.println ("value ="+t.x);
        }
}
Output: value=2
```

Q   **How would you make a copy of an entire Java *object* with its state?**

A   By implementing a *Cloneable* interface and invoking its method *clone()*.

Q   **What interface must be implemented before it can be written to a stream as an object?**

A   *Serializable* or *Externalizable* interface.

Q   **What is meant by *StreamTokenizer*?**

A   *StreamTokenizer* splits up *InputStream* into tokens that are delimited by sets of characters.

Q   **What is a *Stream*?**

A   A *Stream* is an abstraction that either constructs or consumes information. There are two stream types known as Byte Streams and Character Streams.
Byte Streams handles bytes of input and output stream and Character Streams handles character of input and output stream.

Q   **What is meant by time slicing or time-sharing?**

A   This is the method of distributing CPU time to individual threads in a priority schedule.

Q   **Which method is used to find the class of an object?**

A   Use *getClass()* method on a given Object to find out what class it belongs. This method is defined in the Object class and is available to all objects.

Q   **Why you want to call super explicitly?**

A   If you want to invoke a parent constructor which has parameters, then *super* needs to use explicitly.

Q   **Q What is mutable and un-mutable strings ?**

A   If the contents of an instance cannot be altered, then it will is called as *Immutable*
Example: String str="Hi";
Strings are always *Immutable.*
    If the content of an instance is modifiable, then it is called as *Mutable.*
Example: StringBuffer str= new StringBuffer("Hi");
StringBuffer contains an array of characters but it is not same as a *String.* The *StringBuffer* is mutable

Chapter 2

Differences

In this section, listed out some of the key differences among Java-7/8 functions and/or keywords.

1. Difference between: *extends* and *implements*

Extends	Implements
Related to single class inheritance, *extends* is for classes.	Related to interface, *implements* is for interfaces.
A class cannot implement a class.	Interface cannot implement interface.
Class extends class	Class implements interface and interface can extend another interface
Inheritance does one class to inherit the properties of another class.	*implements* builds up to implement the methods declared in the interface.
By using *extends* you can only extend one class in Java at a time.	But by using *implements* you can implement many interfaces at a time.
When you are using a *extends* class, any methods that you write with the same name will override the super class method.	When you are using *implements* a class, the parent class had nothing more than the method declaration (i.e. there was no code in the method). Therefore you are adding your own method code to what was just a method declaration in the interface but not overriding the parent methods instead you just filling up the method.

Similarities between:*extends* and *implements*
a. Both *implements* and *extends* create subtypes.

2. Difference between: *Imports, Implements* and *Inheritance*

Imports	Implements	Inheritance

| It is used to import already compiled libraries. e.g: *import java.util.Random;* Imports are generally coded at the beginning or top of your code. | In Java object-oriented program (OOPs), a class cannot inherit from multiple classes. Therefore at any instance of time, only one class can be super class. But you can implement more than one interface. However, a class can inherit another class and implement an interface at the same time. An interface is a class but it has only signature of methods. | Inheritance is a feature of OOPs. It allows code reuse and expansion. |

3. Difference between: *Abstract class* and *Interface*

Properties	Abstract class	Interface
Definition	The methods of this class must always be redefined in a subclass called overriding and defining the methods in subclass is mandatory.	It specifies a set of methods that an instance must handle.
Default behaviour	Instance methods in abstract class can implement a default behaviour.	It cannot be achieved and all methods are implicitly abstract.
Visibility of members	It can have members of private, public, protected or none and also with partial implementation.	It has only public members or none (package) and no implementation.
Inheritance	A class can extend only one abstract class or vice versa.	It provides multiple inheritances. A class can implement several interfaces.
Performance	It is faster compared to interfaces.	It is slow, because it requires extra redirection to find corresponding method in the actual classes.
Abstract or non-abstract methods	This class can have non-abstract methods. Further, non-abstract methods need not be overridden in the subclass.	All methods are implicitly abstract.
Variables	Programmer can declare variables as required (default and instance variables and final variables).	All variables in an interface must be *constants*. They are implicitly declared *public static final*.

Constructor	It can define a constructor.	It cannot define a constructor.
Identity	Classes will determine the behavior of an object.	Interfaces will determine the role of an object.
Constants	You can define both instance and static constants. Both static and instance initializer code can access the constants.	Only static final constants can use them without qualification in classes that implement the interface. This is little confusion when you are using them and it is not obvious where they are coming from since the qualification is optional.
Related or unrelated classes implementation or extends	A third party class must be rewritten to extend from the abstract class.	An interface implementation may be added to any existing third party class.
When best to use?	Abstract class works best, if the various implementations of similar kind and share a common status and behaviour, Abstract classes are useful in a situation where some general methods should be implemented and specialization behaviour should be implemented by child classes.	If all the implementations share the method signatures, then an interface works best. Interfaces are useful in the situations where all properties should be implemented.
Scalability or adding functionality	If a new method is added to an abstract class, it has a default implementation associated. Then all existing code will continue to work without change.	If you add a new method to an interface, you must track down all implementations of that interface and provide them with a concrete implementation of that method.
Static methods	Allowed	Static methods are not allowed. Only *public* or *abstract* modifier are allowed.
Static initializer blocks	Allowed	Not allowed
User defined exceptions	Not allowed to define.	User defined exceptions can be defined within an interface
Keyword	Abstract class is a class prefix with an *abstract* keyword followed by *class* definition.	Interface which starts with *interface* keyword.
When both are same?	If fully abstract class where all methods declared as abstract and all fields are *public static final*, then it is similar to interface.	You cannot achieve similar to abstract class.
Code sharing	Possible	Not allowed

Marker	You can use abstract class also as *abstract*, but it cannot extend any other class.	You can use interface as marker. An interface having no methods is called as a marker interface. Marker is like an indication, which provides intimation to the JAM or Container. For example, we want to store an object in the file then we have to intimate to the compiler that this object should be stored. This intimation can be done by implementing the interface *java.io.Serializable*.
Variable Initialization	Not necessary.	Mandatory.
Defined or derived	In abstract class, methods are derived.	Interfaces are nothing but defined methods.
Relationship	Abstract classes are used only when there is a is-a type of relationship between the classes. With abstract classes, you are grabbing away each class's individuality.	Interfaces can be implemented by classes that are not related to one another. With Interfaces, you are merely extending each classs functionality.
Implementations	If a class is declared to be abstract, it need not implement all of the interface methods.	A class that implements an interface must implement all of the interface's methods.

Similarities between:*Abstract class* and *Interface*
a) Neither abstract class nor interface can be instantiated.
b) Both can have *final* variables.
c) If the client code invokes using interface/abstract only, then you can easily change the concrete implementation behind it using a factory method.

4. Difference between: ***Extending the Thread class* and *Implementing a thread using Runnable interface***

Extending Thread	Runnable Interface
Thread is a class	*Runnable* is an interface.
If a *thread* class to be extended, then you can use *Thread* class.	If a non-thread class need to be extended, then use *Runnable* interface.
You have to implement it as subclass while extending.	A class that implements *Runnable* can run without subclassing. In most of the cases, the *Runnable* interface should be used if you are only planning to override the *run()* method and no other *Thread* methods.
A sub-class of *Thread* cannot extend any other type. So application specific code should be added rather than inheriting.	A new class can be a subclass of any class and implements *Runnable* interface.

Extending a *Thread* class you can have the facility of overriding the *start()* method.	Implementing the *Runnable* interface will only give you option of implementing the *run* method. If you need to complete the control over *Thread*, then extend the *Thread* class other wise you can choose *Runnable* interface.
A Java *Thread* controls the main path of execution of the application.	The *Runnable* interface defines the class that should be run by the thread.
Separating the *Thread* class from the *Runnable* implementation also avoids potential synchronization problems between the thread and the *run* method.	A separate *Runnable* generally gives greater flexibility in the way that *runnable* code is refered and executed.

Example:
 	
`public class Thread{}`
`        public void run(){`
`    }`
`}`
	Example:
	
	`public interface Runnable{`
	`        public void run();{`
	`        }`
	`}`

Similarities between:**Extending the *Thread* class and implementing a *Thread* using *runnable* interface**
a) Both requires the body of the *run()* method.

5. Difference between: *this* and *super()*

this	*super()*
It is used to invoke a constructor of the same class.	It is used to invoke a *super* class constructor.
Refers to the current object instance.	It is used to refer to the variables and methods of the *super* class from the current object instance.

Similarities between:*this* and *super()*
a) Both are used to invoke the constructor. b) Should be first statement in the constructor.

6. Difference between: *PATH* and *CLASSPATH*

PATH	CLASSPATH
PATH is an environment variable which is used by the OS to find the executable files.	CLASSPATH is an environment variable which is used by the Java compiler to find the path of classes or path of jar files.
PATH is nothing but setting up an environment for OS. The OS will look in this PATH for executables.	CLASSPATH is nothing but setting up the environment for Java where it finds the compiled classes.
PATH refers to the system while CLASSPATH refers to the development environment.	CLASSPATH set path of jars for compiling classes.

7. Difference between: *Abstract Class* and *Abstract Method*

Abstract Class	Abstract Method
This is a class that is declared as *abstract*. It may or may not include abstract methods.	An *abstract* method is one that is declared without an implementation. (i.e. without braces and followed by a semicolon).
Abstract classes cannot be instantiated but they can be sub classed.	Abstract methods always filled in subclasses.
When an abstract class is subclassed, the subclass usually provides implementations for all the abstract methods in its parent class. However, if it does not, the subclass must also be declared as *abstract*.	Abstract method is overridden by the full method definitions contained in the sub-classes.
An abstract class does not have to contain an abstract method or abstract properties. However, a class that does contain at least one abstract method or abstract properties is considered to be an abstract class. Therefore it should be identified using the keyword *abstract* (otherwise it will not compile). Similarly, an abstract class can contain methods or abstract properties that are not abstract.	Abstract method can be declared in abstract class or non abstract class. Any class with an abstract method is automatically abstract. Thus it should be declared *abstract*.
Attempting to instantiate an object of an abstract class results in a compilation error.	An abstract method in Java is something like a pure virtual function in C++ (i.e., a virtual function that is declared = 0).

Similarities between:*Abstract Class* and *Abstract Method*
a) All methods in an interface are implicitly abstract. So the *abstract* modifier is not used with interface methods.

8. Difference between: *abstract* and *final*

property	*abstract*	*final*
Subclassing	Should be subclassed to override the functionality of abstract methods.	Can never be subclassed as final does not permit.
Method alterations	The functionality of methods of abstract class can be altered in the subclass.	Final class methods should be used as it is by other classes.
Overriding concept	All the abstract methods should be overridden for later use.	Final class cannot be inherited.

Inheritance	Can be inherited.	Cannot be inherited.
Instantiation	Cannot be instantiated.	Can be instantiated.
Abstract methods	Can have abstract methods.	Cannot have abstract methods.
Partial implementation	Few methods can be implemented and a few cannot.	All methods must have implementation.
Nature	It is an incomplete class.	It is a complete class.
Adding extra functionality	Extra functionality to the methods can be added in subclass.	No extra functionality can be added and should be used as it is.
Immutable objects	Cannot create immutable objects (also, no objects can be created).	Immutable objects can be created (e.g. String class).

9. Difference between: *Object* **and** *Object reference*

Object	Object Reference
Class instantiation is called instance of a class.	The created object's address is referred by a variable.
It specifies the state and/or behaviour.	The whole object is identified by the reference.
For example: *Bird b = new Bird("pigeon",2);* Here *new Bird("pigeon",2);* is called dynamic object creation. Objects don't have names. It has types and locations in memory along with fields and methods. The above statement creates a *new Bird* object in memory, initializing it with the data received as arguments to the constructor.	For example: *Bird b = new Bird("pigeon",2);* When object created, reference of the object *Bird* is assigned to the variable *b*. It is a reference or object type variable which can reference a *Bird* object or subclass of *Bird*.
An object may contain references to other objects.	At any moment, it provides one reference for one object only. A reference object encapsulating the reference to another object is known as referent.
The garbage collector identifies objects that are no longer in use and reclaims the memory or resources allocated.	The referent of a reference object is specified when the reference object is created. If the garbage collector collects a weakly reachable object, all weak references are set to *null*. So that the referent object can no longer be accessed through the weak reference.

Similarities between:*Object* **and** *Object Reference*
a) Subclass variable can't reference a superclass object, but only superclass variable can reference a

subclass object. Example: All pigeons are birds but all birds are not pigeons.

b) A program can use a reference queue to create a circumstances, where the program is notified when a certain object is reachable only through reference objects. Upon notification, the program can proceed with clean-up operations on other related objects to make them eligible for garbage collection.

c) An object is in use if it can be accessed or reached by the program in its current state.

10. Difference between: **Single threading** and **Multi-threading**

Single threading	Multi-threading
A single threaded program contains only one part and runs sequentially.	A multi-threaded program contains 2 or more parts that run concurrently.
Single tasking	Multitasking
Thread synchronization is not required. Hence monitors and mutexes are not required.	Requires thread synchronization. Monitors and mutexes are used for synchronization.
Less processing overhead.	More processing overhead compared to single thread. Multi-threading differs from multiprogramming. Multi-threading provides concurrency within the context of a single process and multiprogramming provides concurrency between processes. However, multi-threading also requires less processing overhead than multiprogramming because concurrent threads are able to share common resources more easily and efficiently.
Less performance compare to multi-threading.	Improves performance.

Similarities between:*Single Threading* and *Multi-threading*
a) A thread is part of a program that is running.

b) A thread can be in one of the following four states:

- Running: Thread is currently executing or processor is allocated.
- Suspended: Execution is paused and may be resumed where it left off.
- Blocked: A thread is waiting for resource currently being used by another thread.
- Terminated: Execution is stopped and cannot be resumed.

All threads are of not equal priority. Some threads are more important than other threads and are given higher priority for the resources such as the CPU, memory, etc. Each thread is assigned a priority that is used to determine the context switching.

c) Threads priority can be assigned using MIN_PRIORITY (1), MAX_PRIOIRTY (10) or NORM_PRIOIRTY (5).

d) If a thread with a higher priority encounters a thread with lower priority for a resource, the lower priority thread will be suspended until the higher priority thread is finished with the resource. Further, if two threads of equal priority demand for the same resource, a thread that request the resource first will be provided. However, the management of threads of same priority depends on the operating system under which the program is running.

For example: Some operating systems forces the first thread to give the second thread access to the resource after a specified time period. This is to ensure that one thread does not hold a resource and prevent other threads from utilizing.

f) Thread priorities are used when context switching are performed. However, following rules are used for determining:

- A thread can voluntarily complete its execution. Eventually, the control is handed over to the highest priority thread.

- A higher priority thread can preempt a lower priority thread for use of a resource.

- Threads of equal priority are processed based on the rules of the operating system. For example, windows uses round robin scheduling for CPU sharing across threads. In Solaris, the second high-priority thread must wait for the first thread to stop.

11. Difference between: *Overloading* **and** *Overriding*

Overloading	Overriding
Another method in the same class having the same method name, but with different arguments.	A method in a subclass with same method name and same arguments as in the super class.
Method signatures are different.	Method signature is same.
It is a relationship between methods available in the same class.	It is a relationship between methods in super class method and subclass.
Separate methods share the same name.	Subclass method replaces the super class method.
Methods with same name co-exists in same class but they must have different method signature.	Signature remains exactly same including return type.
"is a" relationship.	"has a" relationship.
Does not block inheritance from the super class.	Does blocks inheritance from the super class.
Static or early binding polymorphism.	Dynamic or late binding polymorphism.
Simply involves having a method with the same name within the class.	You can change the method behaviour in the derived class.
Overloaded methods are independent methods of a class and can invoke each other just like any other method.	Overriding methods maintains relationship between super class and subclass. It can call the overriding method in super class using keyword *super*.
Constructors can also be overloaded in the similar fashion.	Cannot override constructors.
Overloading is generally used while implementing several methods that implement similar behaviour but for different data types.	The method in the super class is said to be overridden by the method in the subclass. Overriding method actually replaces the super class method with subclass method.

Any visibility is allowed on overloading methods.	Methods overriding cannot be declared more private than the super class method. In other words the overriding method may not limit the access of the method it overrides.
You can declare overloading method as *final*.	Methods declared as *final* cannot be overridden. An overriding method declared as final using keyword *final* suggest that this method cannot be further overridden.
Private method overloading is allowed.	Methods declared as *private* cannot be overridden as they are not visible outside the class.
Method calling is achieved through object.	Overriding method can call the overridden method (just like any other method) in its super class with keyword *super*. *super.method()* will invoke the method of immediate super class. Though keyword *super* is used to refer super class, method call *super.super.method()* is invalid.
Overloaded methods need not have the same list of thrown exceptions.	The overriding method should throw same exceptions that are thrown by the overridden method. In other words any exceptions declared in overriding method must be of the same type as those thrown by the super class, or a subclass of that type.
Static overloading methods are allowed.	Static overriding methods are not allowed.

12. Difference between: *Instance, Object, Reference* and *Class*

Instance	Object	Reference	Class

An instance should have a class definition. Example: *Student S = new Student();* Where *S* is an instance.	An object is an instance of a class. We can create object in different ways as follows, • Using *new* operator • Using *class.forName*: *Classname obj = Class.forName("Fully Qualified class Name").newInstance();* • Using *this.getClass().getClassLoader() .loadClass(com.abc.Test).newInstance();* • Using *object.clone* • Using *ObjectInputStream obj =new ObjectInputStream(inputStream);* *Test obj1 = (Test) obj.readObject();.*	A reference is just like a pointer pointing to an object.	Class is a user defined data type with set of data members and member functions.
This represents the values of data members of a class at a particular instant.	An object is an instance of a class.	*Student S = new Student();* Returns a reference of *Student* object to the *Student* instance.	Class is a template for objects.

13. Difference between: *""(empty string)* and *null*

property	empty string(*""*)	Null
String	It is a String.	Need not be a String.
.length()	*""*.length() results in 0.	null.length() results in Null-PointerException.
.equals	*""*.equals(null) returns false because *""* is not equal to null.	null.equals(*""*) results in Null-PointerException.

14. Difference between: *Literals* and *Variables*

Literals	Variables
Mentioning truth or actual value.	On demand value generating.
Static value.	Dynamic value.
It could be a constant value.	Values can be varied.
e.g.: *int i = 10;* here 10 is a literal.	e.g.: *int i=k*m*n;* here *k,m* and *n* are variables .

Similarities between:*Literals* **and** *Variables*
Allows all data types of literals and variables.

15. Difference between: *Local, Instance* **and** *Class Variables*

Questions	Local variable (method or block variables)	Instance variable (member variables)	Class variable (Static variables)
How to Define?	These are declared inside a method, constructor or block. Local variables are not visible outside the method or block. When the method is called, memory is allocated to the local variables. When the method exits, the memory allocated to the local variables is removed and claimed back to memory heap.	These are declared inside the class, but outside the methods. An instance variable is created when an object is created and destroyed when the object is destroyed. When an object is allocated memory from heap, memory is allocated for all class variables.	These are variables declared with the *static* keyword in a class, but outside a method. Only one copy per class are created regardless of how many objects are created. They are stored in static memory. When the object is destroyed, the memory allocated to static variables is not removed.
What is the lifetime ?	Created when method or constructor is invoked. Destroyed on exit.	Created when the instance of class is created with *new* keyword. Destroyed when there are no more references to enclosing object (made available for garbage collection).	Created when the program starts. Destroyed when the program stops.
Where is it used ?	To do temporary or local computations inside the method or block.	These are essential parts of an object's state. Instance variables hold values that would be accessed by methods.	Widely used for variables whose value or state to be continued throughout the life of the class.
What is scope/visibility ?	Local variables/formal parameters are visible within the method or constructor or block in which they are declared.	Instance variables (fields) can been accessed by all methods in the class.	Similar to instance variable, but are often declared public to make available to users of the class.
Where it could be declared ?	Block, method and constructor.	Inside class and outside a method.	Inside class (declared with *static* keyword).

Where to do declaration ?	Anywhere in a method or block, but it has to be declared before it is used.	Anywhere at class level.	Anywhere at class level with *static*.
How to access from outside ?	Not possible to access outside of block-/method.	Instance variables are basically used for information hiding, hence it is usually being declared as private, therefore can not be accessed from outside a class. However to access from outside the class, they must be qualified by an object (eg, Test.t).	These variables are qualified with the class name. They can also be qualified with an object.
What is initial value ?	There is no defined value. Must be assigned a value before the first use.	0(Zero)/false/*null* for numbers, booleans and object respectively. Can be assigned value at declaration or in constructor.	Similar to instance variable and in addition, the value can be assigned in the special static initializer block.

16. Difference between: *Abstract Method* **and** *Static Method*

Abstract method	Static method
Abstract class cannot be instantiated. Abstract methods always implemented in subclasses.	No need to instantiate a class (including abstract by extending etc.) in order to call a *static* method.
Abstract method can be declared in abstract class or non-abstract class. Any class having an abstract method is abstract class. So class should also be declared abstract. A subclass of an abstract class can be instantiated only if it overrides each of the abstract methods of its superclass and provides method body for all of the methods. Such a class is generally known as concrete subclass.	Methods or Variables marked *static* belong to the class rather than to any particular instance of the class. These methods or variables can be used without having any instances of that class at all. Only the class name is sufficient to invoke a static method or access a static variable.
An abstract method can be declared without an implementation (without braces and followed by a semicolon) and can be defined in the subclass.	Static methods can't be overridden. They can be redefined in a subclass (redefining and overriding are not the same thing). It is known as Hiding.

The static, private and final methods cannot be abstract. Since these types of methods cannot be overridden by a subclass. Similarly, a final class cannot contain any abstract methods.	A static method cannot access non-static/instance variables, because a static method is never associated with any instance.
An abstract class may have static fields and static methods. You can use these static members with a class reference.	Static method can access non-static methods by using instances. By definition, a non-static method is one that is called on instance of some class, whereas a static method belongs to the class itself.

17. Difference between: *Java compiler* and *Java interpreter*

Java compiler	Java interpreter
It is a program, which translates Java language's source code into the Java Virtual Machine (JVM) bytecodes after compiling a program.	It is a program, which implements the JVM specification and actually executes the bytecodes while running the program.
Command: javac program_name.java	Command: java program_name
Generates class file while compiling.	Executes class (Java byte-code) file which is generated by Java compiler.
Java compiler reads entire program and checks for errors, then compiles it.	Just-In-Time compiler (or JIT compiler) is a part of a JVM. Its purpose is to take the generic (i.e. cross-platform) bytecodes and compile them into more machine-specific instructions.

18. Difference between: *Java Compiler* and *Java Decompiler*

Java compiler	Java decompiler
It is a program, which translates Java language's source code into the Java Virtual Machine (JVM) bytecodes after compiling the program.	It is a program that translates from a low level (generally bytecode) to a higher level source code (human readable class form).

19. Difference between: *final, finalize* and *finally*

final	finalize	finally

Final is a modifier and this keyword is used for constant declaration.	This keyword is used for garbage collection. *finalize* is used just before object deletion for garbage collection.	This keyword is used in exception handling. The *finally* block always executes soon after control exits from *try* block. This ensures that the finally block is executed even if an unexpected exception occurs while running the program. It allows the developer to avoid having cleanup code accidentally bypassed by either *return, continue* or *break*.
The *final* variable acts like a constant. This value can't be changed from its initiated value. The final method can't be overridden. The *final* class cannot be subclassed.	This function can not be used to release non memory resources like file handles, sockets, database connections etc., because Java has only a finite number of these resources and it is not defined when the garbage collection is going to release these non-memory resources through the *finalize()* method.	The function of *finally* will not be executed if you use *System.exit(0)* call. *finally* is a closed exception statement.
A final class implicitly has all the methods as final, but not necessarily the data members. A *final* class may not be extended or final method be overridden.	The finally block code is guaranteed of execution irrespective of occurrence of exception. Whereas for finalize it is not guaranteed. The *finalize* method is called by the garbage collector on an object when the garbage collector determines that there are no more references to the object.	Basically finally block is used to release resources irrespective of exceptions. It will be executed whether or not *try* block executes.

20. Difference between: *println* **and** *Print*

println	Print
Adds a new line at the end of printed line and places a cursor on new line.	Print out the line and the cursor is placed immediately after the printed line.

The next display will automatically start on the new line.	Does not perform a carriage return.

21. Difference between: *Constructor* and *Default Constructor*

Constructor	Default Constructor
Similar to methods which has same name as class. Constructor does not have return statement or return type. When a new instance (a new object) of a class is created using *new* keyword, a constructor for that class is invoked. Generally, it is used to initialize the instance variables (fields) of the object.	It is a constructor that is automatically generated in the absence of explicit constructors or defined constructor. If you don't define a constructor for a class, the compiler automatically creates a default parameterless constructor. The default constructor calls the default parent constructor (*super()*) and initializes all instance variables to default value (zero for numeric types, null for object references and false for booleans). Default constructor is created only if there are no constructors. If a constructor is defined for the class, then default constructor is not created.
The first line of a constructor must either be a call on to another constructor in the same class (using this operator), or a call to the *super* class constructor (using *super* method). If the first line is neither of these, the compiler automatically inserts a call to the parameterless *super* class constructor. *this* operator can be used invoke another constructor in the same class. *super()* can be used to call a constructor of a parent class.	This default constructor will call the no argument constructor of the super class. In this case, the compiler will throw error if the super class doesn't have a no argument constructor. So it should be verified for the existence before invoking no argument constructor. If your class has no explicit super class, then it has an implicit super class of *Object*, which does have a no-argument constructor. A default constructor is called as *nullary* constructor and does not take any arguments.

22. Difference between: *Vector, Array* and *Arraylist*

Vector	*Array*	*Arraylist*
Vector can be grown or shrink as required	Array cannot be grown or shrink.	*Arraylist* can be grown or shrink.
It is implemented from *List* interface.	Arrays can be any of the primitive data types or reference types.	It is implemented from *List* interface.

Vector is *synchronized*.	Not *synchronized*.	*Arraylist* is not *synchronized*. But can be synchronized manually.
Vector performance is not as good as *Arraylist*.	*Array* has best performance than *Vector* and *Arraylist*.	For better performance use *Arraylist* than *Vector*.
Vector defaults to doubling the size of its array. *Vector* can hold objects of different data type .	*Array* size is fixed. *Array* can hold similar data type elements.	*ArrayList* increases its array size by 50%.

23. Difference between: *String, StringBuffer* and *StringBuilder*

String	StringBuffer	StringBuilder
Immutable / constant	Mutable	Mutable
Asynchronized	Synchronized	Asynchronized
StringBuffer is faster than *String* for simple operations like concatenations. *String* is generally lighter and faster and recommended for use if *String* is not modified.	*StringBuilder* is more efficient than *StringBuffer*.	*StringBuilder* is more efficient than *StringBuffer*.
If the text / data does not modify in the program, *String* class is recommended because *String* object is immutable.	If your text / data changes and is accessed from multiple threads, *StringBuffer* is recommended because *StringBuffer* is synchronous.	If the text data changes and will be accessed by single thread only, then use *StringBuilder* because *StringBuilder* is asynchronized.

Similarities between:*String, StringBuffer* and *StringBuilder*
All are *final* classes.

24. Difference between: *String* and *StringBuffer*

Features	String (Asynchronous and final class)	StringBuffer (Synchronous and final class)

Compare	+equals(s1: String): boolean +equalsIgnoreCase(s1: String): boolean +compareTo(s1: String): int +compareToIgnoreCase(s1: String): int +startsWith(prefix: String): boolean +endsWith(suffix: String): boolean	Note: StringBuilder(Asynchronous and final class), All operations in StringBuilder are same as StringBuffer.
Length and ChatAt	+length(): int +charAt(index: int): char	+length()
Concatenate	+concat(s1: String): String Str1+str2: String	+append(boolean b) +append(char c) +append(char[] str) +append(char[] str, int offset, int len) +append(double d) +append(float f) +append(int i) +append(long l) +append(Object obj) +append(String str)
Substring	+subString(beginIndex: int): String +subString(beginIndex: int, endIndex: int): String	+substring(int start) +substring(int start, int end)
Replacing or delete	+replace(oldChar: char, newChar: char): String +replaceFirst(oldString: String, newString: String): String +replaceAll(oldString: String, newString: String): String	+delete(startIndex: int, endIndex: int): StringBuilder +deleteCharAt(index: int): StringBuilder +insert(offset: int, data: char[]): StringBuilder +insert(offset: int, b: aPrimitiveType): StringBuilder +insert(offset: int, s: String): StringBuilder +replace(startIndex: int, endIndex: int, s: String): StringBuilder +setCharAt(index: int, ch: char): void
Converting, trim and Splitting Strings	+toLowerCase(): String +toUpperCase(): String +trim(): String +split(delimiter: String): String[]	
Matching with EL	replaceAll, replaceFirst, split, matches	

Index of char/substr	+indexOf(ch: char): int +indexOf(ch: char, fromIndex: int): int +indexOf(s: String): int +lastIndexOf(ch: int): int +lastIndexOf(s: String): int	+indexOf(String str) +indexOf(String str, int fromIndex) +lastIndexOf(String str) +lastIndexOf(String str, int fromIndex)
Numbers /buff to String	String s = "" + num; String s = Integer.toString (i); String s = Double.toString (d); String s = String.valueOf (num);	+toString ();
Reverse		+reverse(): StringBuilder

25. Difference between: *Class* and *Interface*

Class	Interface
A class is a group of methods and variables.	An interface provides signatures of the methods. Unlike classes, interfaces do not provide their definitions. Classes define all methods.
The class automatically extends the class Object.	By default all methods are abstract. Hence, do not use *abstract* keyword before the *abstract* method.

26. Difference between: *start() in a thread* and *run() in a thread*

start()	run()
Invokes the execution of this threads. The JVM calls the *run* method of current thread.	If the current thread is based on separate *Runnable* run object, then the *Runnable* object's *run* method is invoked. Otherwise, current method does nothing and returns.
The *start()* method will create a new *thread* and code inside *run()* method is executed in this *thread*.	If *run()* method is invoked, new *thread* is not created, rather the code inside *run()* method will execute on current *thread*.

27. Difference between: *Multiprocessing* and *Multithreading*

Multiprocessing	Multithreading
More than one job can run at same time.	Same job would be segmented logically and executed simultaneously and the results from each segment are combined.
Using a computer that has multiple processors (CPUs).	The OS can allow many threads to be active, regardless of the number of processors. It depends on OS to share the processor time among various threads.
Computer has more than one processor and each thread will be handled by a different processor. Hence leading to concurrent processing of tasks.	Though it appears to be concurrent processing to the end user, internally only one thread is executing. Processor is able to multitask by switching between the threads.
Each processes execution is independent of other. Any error in one of the process does not impact the execution of another process. Each processes may belong to different users and have different privileges.	Any error or problem in one thread can impact all the other threads in the process. A thread is a "light weight" approach of concurrency. However, it is a stream of instructions within a process. Further, each thread has its own instruction pointer (IP), registers and stack memory. But, the virtual address space is same to all threads within a process. So, data on the heap can be readily accessed by all threads.

28. Difference between: *Compile time errors* **and** *Run time errors*

Compile time errors	Run time errors
Mostly determines syntax errors.	An error, which happens while running a program.
Error may be due to the structure of Java language.	Runtime errors are due to logical errors.
Example: Missing data type for a variable.	Example: A number divides zero.
Common mistakes: Syntax errors or semantic errors. Type checking errors.	Common mistakes: Casting a null value. Running out of memory. Trying to access a file that is not there.

29. Difference between: *Errors* **and** *Exceptions*

Errors	Exceptions

Generally, error refers to compile time error. Example: Can't convert *xxx* to *Boolean*.	Runtime error is called an exception. Example: An *ArithmeticException* is a *RuntimeException*. An *ArithmeticException* is a recoverable error.
Errors that can't be handled by the JVM will to lead to termination of the program. It needs to be corrected in source code.	These errors are in the scope of JVM and can be handled using *try-catch* block. A checked exception is something that might be captured at runtime and can be handled appropriately.
The error class defines error conditions that should not attempted to recover. It is advisable to terminate when such an error is encountered.	The exception class defines mild error conditions that the program encounters. Exceptions can occur when trying to open the file, which does not exist or operands being manipulated are out of prescribed ranges or the class file you are interested in loading is missing, etc..

Similarities between:***Errors*** **and** ***Exceptions***
a). *Exception* and *Error* is sub class of *Throwable*.

30. Difference between: ***try/catch/throw*** **and** *try/catch(e)/throw e*

try/catch/throw	try/catch(e)/throw e

Syntax :
try { }
catch {
throw;
}
	Syntax:
	try { }
	catch (Exception e) {
	throw e;
	}

The current exception is thrown again and that exception will keep its "source" and stack trace.	When exception is thrown the source and stack trace is changed. An exception can be thrown from the current method.

Similarities between:*try/catch/throw* and *try/catch(e)/throw e*
It will catch every exception thrown inside the *try* block.

31. Difference between: ***Instance method*** **and** ***Class method***

Instance method	Class method
An instance method is a regular method of an instantiated class. In other words, the methods of the instantiated object of a class.	A class method is a *static* method. It is called using the class name.

| A class method is associated with a particular object instance. It has 'this' reference. | A class method is not associated with a particular object instance. It does not have a 'this' reference. |
| Instance of a class is created using *new* keyword. | Declared with the keyword *static*. |

32. Difference between: *int* and *Integer*

int	Integer
The *int* is a primitive data type. It is not an object. However, every primitive data type has its own wrapper class like *Float, Double, Boolean, Long, Character* and *Short*.	It is an object that contains a single *int* field. Howevver, *Integer* owns a wrapper class and it is a non-primitive data type.
Performance using *int* is high and is streamlined best for calculating numbers in the range $-2,147,483,648[-2^{31}]$ aka *Integer*(32 bits OS).	An *Integer* is of relatively low performance compared to than *int*.
int variables are mutable, unless it is declared *final*.	*Integers* are immutable. If you want to affect the value of an *Integer* variable, an approach to modify is to create a new *Integer* object and discard the old one.
No explicit package.	Use following package: *java.lang.Integer*.
You can not store it in a *Vector* or other collection. Cannot use it as a *HashMap* key.	You can store it in a *Vector* or other collection. You can use it as a *HashMap* key.
No serialize	Serialize
The *null* value is not allowed.	The *null* value is allowed which means there is no value.
Considering performance, primitive data types are faster than *Wrapper* class objects.	Non primitive data types are relatively slower than primitive data types.

Similarities between:*int* and *Integer*
a. Can be passed as a parameter.
b. You can return as a value.
c. Can be used as argument of another object over RMI.
d. Can operate using arithmetic operators $(+, -, *, /, \%)$ and $\wedge$.

33. Difference between: *Mutable Objects* and *Immutable Objects*

Mutable Objects	Immutable Objects

When you have a reference to an instance of an object, the contents of that instance can be altered. e.g., *stringbuffer obj*	When you have a reference to an instance of an object, the contents of that instance cannot be altered. e.g,.*String obj*

34. Difference between: *Java* **and** *JavaScript*

Java	JavaScript
Java is a object oriented programming language.	JavaScript is object oriented programming scripting language.
Java creates applications that run in a virtual machine or browser. It can execute on its own	JavaScript code can run on a browser only. In other words, javascript must be placed inside an HTML document for execution.
Java is much larger and robust programming language to generate "standalone" applications.	JavaScript is text that is fed into a browser that can read it and then is enacted by the browser.
Java must be compiled into "machine language" before it can execute on the Web.	Javascript should be placed in an HTML document and it will run through a browser. You can modify it after completion of execution and then execute the modified script.
Compiled on server side before execution on client.	Interpreted (not compiled) by client/browser.
Variable data types must be declared (strong typing).	Variable data types not declared (loose typing).
Static binding. Object references must exist at compile time.	Dynamic binding. Object references are looked upon at run time.

Similarities between:*Java* **and** *JavaScript*
Both are OOP based languages.

35. Difference between: *Throw, Throws* **and** *Throwable*

Throw	Throws	Throwable
The keyword *throw* is used to throw user defined exceptions.	The keyword *throws* is used for method signatures to declare that the current method would possibly throw an exception.	Throwable is an interface that the *Exception* class implements and all user defined class would implicitly implement an interface to ensure that they have exception like behavior.

A *throw* statement requires single argument. That is a instance of any subclass of the *Throwable* class. Executing *throw* statement triggers the JVM to throw this exception and causes an exception to occur.	For checked exceptions, the compiler will guarantee the code invoking that method must catch these checked exceptions.	All errors and exceptions classes are derived from *java.lang.Throwable* class. Only objects that are instances of this class (or one of its subclasses) are thrown by JVM or can be thrown by *throw* statement.

36. Difference between: *Runnable* **and** *Thread*

Runnable	Thread
Runnable is the interface. To run threads, class has to either extend *Thread Class* or has to implement *Runnable* interface.	*Thread* is a class, used to create threads. Class *Thread* implements *Runnable*.
Runnable interface is used to create simple threads and does not need any modifications such as adding new functionality or improving behaviors	Thread class is used when any modification on *Thread* is required.
Runnable interface contains *run*() method to start the action without any argument.	While extending a thread class, the subclass will have all functionalities of thread, however when you creating a thread using runnable interface, then you need to pass this object to thread class to have all functionalities of thread.

37. Difference between: *Arithmetic Exception* **and** *Number Format Exception*

Arithmetic exception	Number format exception
Thrown when an exceptional arithmetic condition has occurred. For example, an integer "divide by zero" throws an arithmetic exception.	*NumberFormat* is the abstract base class for all number formats. This class provides the interface for formatting and parsing numbers. *NumberFormat* also provides methods for determining which locales have number formats and what are their names. If there is violation of format, then *NumberFormat* exception is raised.

Similarities between:*Arithmetic exception* **and** *Number format exception*
Both are un-checked exception.

38. Difference between: *'is a' Relationship* **and** *'has a' Relationship*

'is a' relationship	'has a' relationship
'is a' relationship is expressed with inheritance .	'has a' relationship is known as composition or aggregation.
Example: House is a building.	Example: House has a bathroom.
Inheritance is uni-directional. For example: House is a building. But building is not a house.	Composition simply means using instance variables that refer to other objects. The class *House* will have an instance variable.
Have to use keyword *extends* and has advantage of code reusability	No need of specific keyword.

Similarities between:*'is a' Relationship* **and** *'has a' Relationship*
Both inheritance and composition allow you to place sub-objects inside your new class.

39. Difference between: *final class* **and** *abstract class*

final class	*abstract* class
Final class is a class which can't be subclassed.	Abstract class should be sub-classed. Abstract class can contain both abstract methods and non-abstract methods.
Final class must be used without any modification.	Sub-class of the abstract class is used.
We can create object.	We cannot create object and cannot be instantiated.
final Class cannot be overridden.	Abstract methods must be overridden when used by subclass. It usually defines some default implementations and provides some tools useful for a full implementation.
Final class cannot be extended and cannot be inherited.	Abstract class can be extended.

40. Difference between: *Call by value* **and** *Call by reference*

Call by value	Call by reference
Java supports only call by value.	Java doesn't pass methods arguments by reference.
Primitive types passed in the method call to push their values on stack and hence called as called by values.	All objects passed to any method call, pass their reference on stack and hence called as called by reference.

Any changes it makes to those values have no effect on the caller's variables.	The object reference itself is passed by value and so both the original reference and parameter copy refer to the same object.

41. Difference between: *Regular API* and *Deprecated API*

Regular API	Deprecated API
Application programming interface (API) is a library of functions that provides tasks like file transfer, networking and data structures.	Indicates API changes from useful to useless state. This is used to inform the developer that they are using an outdated or non-exising class or methods. When invoked or accessed, the compiler will warn it as invalid usage. Deprecated class, interface, constructor, method or field may be available currently for use, but not suggested for use, as may stop to exist in a future version.

42. Difference between: *Object creation* and *Object destruction*

Object creation	Object destruction
Object is created using an allocation expression. E.g. *newInstance()* methods of the Class or *java.lang.reflect.Constructor* class can be used to create an instance of a class. In both cases, the storage needed for the object is allocated by the system.	In Java, there are no explicit methods to destroy an object instantaneously. However, an object is automatically destroyed when the garbage collector when it determines it is safe remove the object.
When a class is instantiated, a constructor is invoked.	Before an object is destroyed by the garbage collector, *finalize()* method is called. It is similar to a destructor in C++.

43. Difference between: *Cloning objects* and *Assigning objects*

Cloning objects	Assigning objects

If you want to make a local copy of objects, use the *clone()* method to perform the operation. For example: The standard library class *ArrayList* overrides *clone()*. So we can call *clone()* for *ArrayList*.	Basically objects are not values in Java, they are manipulated through references. If one reference is pointing to an object. One more reference can be pointed to same object. Thus, two references point to the same object.

Example:
 	
``
ArrayList a=new ArrayList();
for(int i = 0; i < 10; i++) {
a.add(new Int(i));
}
ArrayList a1 = (ArrayList)
a.clone();
``
	Example:
	
	``
	AAA a = new AAA ();// object a
	//create object of Subclass
	Subclass s=new Subclass();
	a=s;
	``

44. Difference between: *State of an object* and *Behaviour of an object*

State of an object	Behaviour of an object
An object stores its state in the fields (variables).	Exposes its behavior through methods (functions).
Hides internal state and interacts through object's methods, which is known as data encapsulation.	Methods operate on an object's internal state and serves as the primary mechanism for object-to-object communication.
E.g., Dogs have state like name, color, breed, hungry etc.	E.g., Dogs have behaviour like barking, fetching, wagging tail etc.

45. Difference between: *break statement* and *return statement*

break	return
break exits out of the current loop.	*return* exits from the function.
Used in loops and *switch* statement.	Used inside the method.

46. Difference between: *break statement* and *continue statement*

break	continue
break exits out of current loop or block.	Flow of control skips the following statements inside current loop.
Used in loops and *switch* statement.	Used only in loops.

47. Difference between: *Synchronization methods* **and** *Asynchronization methods*

Synchronization methods	Asynchronization methods
Synchronized methods are used to control access of an object. A thread executes a synchronized method after it has acquired the lock for the method's object or class. A synchronized statement will be executed after the thread has acquired the lock for the object or class referenced in the synchronized statement.	Asynchronized methods does not need any control to access the object.
Synchronous action will wait for the action to complete before moving on to the next action.	Asynchronous action does not wait for completion of any action. Asynchronous functions are invoked, but the current code just continues after it starts the function.

48. Difference between: *super* **and** *final*

super	final
The *super* keyword is used to access the methods/variables of the parent class.	The *final* keyword is used to ensure that the methods/variables are not modified/overridden in their child or subclasses.
| Example<br><br>```
public class A extends B {
        super.get();
}
``` | Example<br><br>```
public class A {
public void final get () {
...
}
}
``` |

49. Difference between: *super()* **and** *super.methodName()*

super()	*super.methodName()*
super() can be used to invoke a super class constructor. Super should be used only in the sub classes. *super* is used to point methods of super class.	It is used to override a method of base / parent class. Also, the behavior of base / parent class will be happen along with the custom behavior of subclass / inherited class.

Example:	Example:
| ```
class A{
public String toString(){
super();
}
}
``` | ```
class A{
public String toString(){
String str = super.toString();
}
}
``` |

50. Difference between: *Procedural programming* and *Object-oriented programming*

Procedural	Object-oriented
Programming logic follows certain procedures and the instructions are executed one after another.	Unit of program is object, which is combination of data and methods to handle data.
Data is exposed to the whole program.	Data is accessible within the object and it assures data security.

51. Difference between: *Argument* and *Parameter*

Argument	Parameter
While using methods, values are passed via variables are called arguments.	While defining a method, variables are passed in the method are called parameters.

52. Difference between: *Super class* and *Subclass*

Super class	Subclass
A super class is a class that will be inherited.	Subclass is a class that does the inheriting.
Super class is a base class.	A subclass can inherit the properties of a super class.
Super class can be extended by subclasses.	A subclass can access all the methods and variables of super class. A subclass extends a super class.

53. Difference between: *Process* and *Thread*

Process	Thread
Process is a program in execution.	Thread is a logical segment of executing program.
A process is an OS-level task or service.	A thread runs inside a process and may be virtual or simulated.
Each process has their own separate memory area and need to take more elaborate steps to share resources.	Threads share resources like memory.
Heavyweight system processes.	Lightweight process
A process is an executing instance of a program.	A process may have multiple threads.
Processes are independent to each other and there is no sharing.	Threads are not independent and shares resources of other threads of same process.
Process switching consumes more time.	Thread does not/negligible consume switching time.
Processes have considerable overhead.	Threads have almost no overhead.

54. Difference between: *Serialization* and *Deserialization*

Serialization	Deserialization
Serialization is the process of writing the state of an object to a byte stream.	Deserialization is the process of restoring serialized objects to initial state.

55. Difference between: *Notify* and *NotifyAll*

Notify	NotifyAll
If more than one thread is waiting, *notify()* wakes up one of them. However, we can not specify the thread.	If more than one thread is waiting, *notifyAll()* awakes all of them. The *notifyAll()* is used much more often.
notify() wakes up a single thread which is waiting on the object's lock.	*notifyAll()* wakes up all waiting threads. However, the scheduler decides which one will run.

Similarities between:*Notify* and *NotifyAll*
a) If zero or one thread is waiting on the object, *notify()* and *notifyAll()* do the same.
b) The *notify()* and *notifyAll()* methods are defined in the object class.
c) They can only be used within synchronized code.

56. Difference between: *Overriding fields* and *Hiding fields*

Overriding fields	Hiding fields

Overriding fields (data variables) are hidden, it cannot be overridden. Overriding member are invoked based on the run time type of the object and not based on the declared type.	Binding for fields in Java is always static and hence it's based on the declared type of the object. Private members are neither hidden nor overridden.

57. Difference between: *Overriding Methods* and *Hiding Methods*

Overriding methods	Hiding methods
Overriding methods are from the inherited class. Static methods cannot be overridden and they are hidden. They follow static binding only.	These are private methods and also static binding. They cannot be accessed directly from any other class (including sub classes) except the class which has them. However, hidden doesn't mean that we can't access the members from the subclass, but indirectly we can access them.

58. Difference between: *Static initialization* and *Instance initialization*

Static initialization	Instance initialization
Static methods are accessible anytime from anywhere, you don't need an object to access it. Similarly static variables. Hence the initialized value will be accessible everywhere.	Java automatically initializes all non-local variables with a default value, i.e. 0 or null, even chars. When object is created, its variables are initialized to default value. Then invokes the constructor and the object's variables are initialized.

59. Difference between: *Explicit constructor invocation* and *Implicit constructor invocation*

Explicit constructor invocation	Implicit constructor invocation
Explicit constructor invocations appear as the first statement in the body of some other constructor. They invoke a constructor of a superclass, although they may also invoke an alternative constructor of the current class.	If a constructor body does not begin with an explicit constructor invocation and the constructor being declared is not part of the primordial class object, then the constructor body is implicitly assumed by the compiler to begin with a superclass constructor invocation *super()*. The invocation of constructor of its direct superclass that takes no arguments.

60. Difference between: *Transient variable* and *Volatile variable*

Transient variable	Volatile variable
Transient variables are exclude them from serialization process. The value of a transient variable cannot be written into DataStream.	Volatile is similar to temporary variable. However, volatile modifier requests the JVM to access the shared copy of the variable. Thus current value is retrieved.
We can use transient modifier when variable need not to be written out when an instance is serialized. That is, attempting to put a non-serializable variable in a serializable class.	Volatile indicates that the field is used by synchronized threads and the compiler should not attempt to perform optimizations on these variables. If two or more threads access a volatile variable without synchronization (methods or blocks) to access the value, then that variable must be declared volatile to ensure all threads see the current value.

Similarities between:*Transient variable* and *Volatile variable*
a) Both are modifiers and used for declaring variables.

61. Difference between: *Serialization* and *Externalization*

Serialization	Externalization
Serialization is the process by which you write the state of an object into a file.	To produce raw class files uses externalizing.
Serializing is always slower than externalizing.	It is faster. Externalizing gives control over the read/write process by implementing the *readExternal* and *writeExternal* methods of *Externalizable*.
It is meant for default serialization.	It is meant for customized serialization.
Default serialization taken care by JVM and programmer doesnot have any control.	JVM does not have any control, everything takes care by programmer.
The serialization of objects in Java allows you to make a byte sequence from any object that has implemented the *Serializable* interface. Further, it allows you to convert the byte sequence into object. The mechanism does not depend on the operating system. Example: Objects can be transfer over network and restore them at the other side.	The process of serialization can be controlled by implementing the *Externalizable* interface instead of *Serializable*. This interface extends the original *Serializable* interface and adds *writeExternal()* and *readExternal()*. These two methods will be automatically invoked in object's serialization and deserialization and can be used to control the whole process.

62. Difference between: *Access specifier* and *Access modifier*

Access specifier	Access modifier
They are used to set the visibility of a class or variable or a method. Classes can be *public* or *default*. Variables and methods can be *public, private, protected* or *default*. Access ranges from totally accessible to totally inaccessible.	Essential to declare field. You can optionally declare a field with following modifier keywords: *final* or *volatile* and/or *static* and/or *transient*. They are optionally used to declare a field. Access modifiers can be applied for class methods or variables. Classes can have modifier like *abstract*. Methods can be abstract, native, synchronized etc.
The access specifiers of Java are *public, private, protected* or default.	Access modifiers provided by Java are *public, private, protected* or default.

63. Difference between: *Serialization* and *Deserialization*

Serialization	Deserialization
The state of an object is saved to file.	The process of creating the object back from the serialized file to initial state.
The process of saving the object state into output stream.	The process of reversing the object state from output stream.

64. Difference between: *Serialization* and *Marshalling*

Serialization	Marshalling
It is like pass by value. Converting objects to sequences of bits that can be transported to a different VM.	This is like pass by reference. The process that is used by RMI to transfer and pass an object between its stub and skeleton.
It is a process of converting and segmenting the object such that it can be sent across the network (bytes).	Process of encoding object to put them on the network. The marshalling process is achieved using object serialization.

65. Difference between: *Public static* and *Private static*

Public static	Private static

Accessible to members of any class.	Cannot invoke the method from outside the class as the method is private to the class.

66. Difference between: *Constructors* and *Methods*

Constructors	Methods
Newly created object fields are initialized. In other words, it sets a state for object.	It will have functionality.
No return type and value.	May have return type and value.
Automatically invoked when an object is created.	Called explicitly.

67. Difference between: *Composition* and *Aggregation*

Composition	Aggregation
It is used to represent a stronger form of ownership.	It is used to signify the ownership or a whole/part relationship.
The composite object has sole responsibility for the nature of its parts in terms of creation and destruction. The composite is dependable for memory allocation and deallocation.	The lifetime of the parts is coincident with whole. The destroy message may not propagate to its components.
E.g: People brain.	E.g.: People vehicle.

68. Difference between: *static* and *final*

static	*final*
Static variable or method is shared by all the instances of objects and it has only one copy.	It is a constant and it cannot be changed.
Static variable can change their values.	Final variables cannot be changed since they are constants.
Static variables are initialized when the class loader loads the class and hence we can access in the static block declaration of the class without declaring an object.	The final variable is only accessible after the declaration of an instance of an object.

Cannot be instantiated. Static variables and methods belongs to the class. Static method cannot be overloaded and overridden.	There can be final variables, methods and classes. Final methods cannot be overridden. Final classes cannot be subclassed.

69. Difference between: *Static inner class (nested class)* **and** *Non static inner class (nested class)*

Static inner class (nested class)	Non static inner class(nested class)
It does not have a reference to a nesting instance. Hence static nested class cannot invoke non-static methods or access non-static fields of an instance of the class within which it is nested.	It has full access to the members of the class within which it has nested i.e both static and non-static members.
Static inner classes does not have object instances.	Non Static inner classes have object instances that are associated with the outer classes.
It can only access the static members of the enclosing class. Further, it is not associated with the instance of the enclosing class and it can have static members only.	Non static class is associated with the instance of the enclosing class. It can access all the members of the enclosing class. It is like other members of the enclosing class.
In static inner class, we can have static declarations.	In non-static inner classes, we cannot have static declarations.
To access static inner class members, no need of outer class reference.	To access non static inner class members, we need outer class reference.

70. Difference between: *Function declarations* **and** *Function definitions*

Function declarations	Function definitions
It gives information about the function like return type, parameters, parameters type, etc.	This tells what the function does.
E.g., void fun (int x, float y);	E.g., void fun(int x,int y) {int z = x + y;}

71. Difference between: *Field declarations* **and** *Field definitions*

Field declarations	Field definitions
Declaring the variable.	Assigning some value to a variable.
Specify the type and no memory is allocated to the variable.	An initial value is assigned and memory is allocated to the variable.

72. Difference between: *const* and *volatile*

const	volatile
This keyword is used to declare the constants i.e the value of this data type will not be changed throughout the program execution.	Used in interrupt-driven and multi-threaded applications. It tells the compiler to always fetch the current value of a variable from memory. It is assumed that it will change frequently.

73. Difference between: *Actual parameters* and *Formal parameters*

Actual parameters	Formal parameters
The actual expression or variable passed to the program when it is called.	The parameter is defined in the parameter list of the function definition and used.
This is also known as arguments which are passed by the caller.	The parameters are known in the function definition.

E.g.,
 	
`int val=111;`
`object.setValue(val);`
`// Here val is actual`
`// parameter.`
	E.g.,
	
	`void setValue(int number){}`
	`//Here number is a formal`
	`// parameter.`

74. Difference between: *Synchronized method* and *Synchronized block*

Synchronized method	Synchronized block
Only one thread can use the method at any given point of time. Hence all requests will be queued and are executed one by one.	Scope of block is smaller than method. Statements in the block are executed sequentially. Synchronized block can lock any monitor (Id can be mentioned) and can have a scope smaller than that of the enclosing method.
It is safe to use for threads. Thread checks object's lock only if we invoke synchronized method.	First, the lock for the reference object inside the block is acquired before method invocation.

Similarities between:*Synchronized method* and *Synchronized block*
Both the synchronized method and block are used to acquires the lock for an object.

75. Difference between: *Synchronized* and *Volatile*

Synchronized	Volatile
Thread checks object's lock only if we invoke synchronized method.	Volatile instructs the compiler not to make assumptions about the data in terms of caching. Such kinds of variables are used in interrupt-driven, memory mapped IO and multithreaded applications.
A thread locks as a critical section in the method to make sure that only one thread at a time may be executing the sections and others must block until it completes the execution.	Read it every time whenever it needs to be read, write it every time whenever it needs to be written.

76. Difference between: *Machine code* and *Byte code*

Machine code	Byte code
Set of instructions written in a format such that the architecture can identify the action to be performed. This is consisting of binary or hexadecimal instructions that a computer can execute it directly.	JAVA compiles the Java file and converts the program into bytecode which is machine independent. Later JVM refers this and converts the bytecodes into machine code. Bytecode is the code which is stored in a *.class* files.

77. Difference between: *Synchronization* and *Serialization*

Synchronization	Serialization
It ensures that only one thread at a time executes a critical block of code.	The process of writing an object's state to an output stream.
Synchronization is a mechanism to restrict the blocks of shared data/code from being accessed by more than one thread at a time.	Serialization is a mechanism for flattening objects to the file or a stream and then reassembling them on the other end or when they are re-instantiated.

78. Difference between: **==** and *equals()*

==	equals()
Used to compare two numbers.	Used to compare two strings.
It can be used to compare the references of the objects.	This method can be overridden for *String* class. The *equals()* method can be used to compare the values of two objects.

This is used to check if two variables point at the same instance of a *String* object.	This is used to compare the values of the *Strings*.
No overriding applies.	On overriding *equals()*, the *hashCode()* method should also be overridden.

79. Difference between: **& and &&**

&	&&
"bit-wise AND" operator	"Conditional logical AND" operator.
Ampercent (&) can be used as Bitwise operator.	AND operation is used for comparison operations.
Evaluates both arguments.	Evaluate the second argument, if the first argument is true.

80. Difference between: **| and ||**

|	||
"bit-wise OR" operator	"Conditional logical OR" operator.
Evaluates both arguments.	Evaluate the second argument if the first argument is false.

81. Difference between: *Comparable interface* **and** *Comparator interface*

Comparable interface	Comparator interface
It has to be implemented by a class to make it comparable.	Comparator could be used to sort a collection by custom sorting.
A comparable object is capable of comparing itself with another object.	A comparator object is capable of comparing two different objects. The class is not comparing its instances, but used to compare some other classes instances.
A class implements the *java.lang.Comparable* interface in order to compare its instances.	A comparator class must implement the *java.lang.Comparator* interface.
It is for natural ordering.	It is for custom ordering. We can override the *compareTo()* method of comparable interface to give a custom ordering.
It uses the *compareTo()* method. Example: *int objectOne.compareTo(objectTwo)*.	It uses *compare()* method. Example: *int compare(ObjOne, ObjTwo)*

It is used to modify the class whose instance is going to be sorted.	A separate class can be created in order to sort the instances.
Only one sort sequence can be created.	Many sort sequences can be created.
The API classes frequently uses it.	It is used by third-party classes to sort instances.

Similarities between:*Comparable interface* **and** *Comparator interface*
Both are used for sorting but in different contexts.

82. Difference between: *Java applet* **and** *Java application*

Java applet	Java application
It is an application that runs on the client's browser when the browser requests a applet embedded.	Servlet is a application that is running on the server. When a server receives a request of a servlet, the server will process the request and provides the result to the client.

83. Difference between: *Web server* **and** *Application server*

Web server	Application server
A web server provides pages for viewing in a web browser.	An application server provides methods for client applications to invoke.
A web server exclusively handles HTTP requests.	Application server provides business logic to the application programs through any number of protocols.

84. Difference between: *Automatic variable* **and** *Static variable*

Automatic variable	Static variable
Local or stack variable	Class variable
Discarded when the method execution completes.	Does not discard when the method execution is completed.

85. Difference between: *Character stream* **and** *Byte stream*

Character stream	Byte stream
Char streams (Reader/Writer) are used for character data.	Byte streams (InputStream/Output-Stream) are used for binary data.

A *char* has a minimum value of \u0000 (or 0) and a maximum value of \uffff (or 65,535 inclusive) and is generally used in Java to represent a character in unicode format.	A byte has a minimum value of −128 and a maximum value of 127 (inclusive).
It is easy to write programs that are not dependent upon a specific character encoding. Therefore easy to internationalize.	It is used to perform input and output of 8-bit bytes.

86. Difference between: *List, Set* and *Map*

List	Set	Map
Collection that has an order associated with its elements.	A collection that has no duplicate elements.	This is a way of storing key and associated value pairs. It is similar to two-column table.

87. Difference between: *Reader/Writer* and *InputStream/Output Stream*

Reader/Writer	InputStream/Output Stream
Character-oriented.	Byte-oriented.
Belongs to the character stream.	Belongs to the byte stream.

88. Difference between: *JRE* and *JDK*

JRE	JDK
Used for running environment	Used for development environment
It is an implementation of the JVM which actually executes Java programs.	It is a bundle of software that you can use to develop Java based applications.
Java Run Time Environment (JRE) is a plug-in needed for running Java programs.	Java Development Kit (JDK) is needed for developing Java applications.
JRE is smaller than JDK. Hence it required less disk space compare to JDK.	JDK needs more disk space as it contains JRE along with various development tools.
It includes JVM, core libraries and other additional components to run applications and applets written in Java.	It includes JRE, API classes, Java compiler, webpages and additional files needed to write Java applets and applications.

89. Difference between: *Iterator* and *Enumeration*

Iterator	Enumeration
Returned by List and other Collection interfaces.	It is used by Vector and Hash table.
It will fail if any modification is performed to the collection while iterating.	Enumeration may or may not throw an error if the collection is changed.

90. Difference between: *HashMap* and *TreeMap*

HashMap	TreeMap
HashMap stores all of its data inside a hash table	A TreeMap stores all of its information in a tree.

91. Difference between: *HashMap* and *Hashtable*

HashMap	Hashtable
HashMap stores all of its data inside a hash table.	It is a concrete implementation of a Dictionary class.
HashMap is not synchronized.	*Hashtable* is synchronized.
Allows *null* values.	Does not allow *null* values.
If you change the iteration, you will get a *java.util.ConcurrentModificationException.*	In *Hashtable*, you can change the iteration and exception will not be thrown.
The iterator in the *HashMap* is fail-safe.	The enumerator for the *Hashtable* is not fail-safe.

92. Difference between: *HashMap* and *HashSet*

HashMap	HashSet
It is not collection interface.	It is collection interface.
Implements *Map* interface.	*HashSet* class implements *Set* interface.
Prints the elements orderly.	Prints the elements without order.
It stores unique keys.	It stores unique elements.
Name and value pair.	No name and value pair.
It belongs to abstract *Map* class.	It belongs to abstract *Set* class.

93. Difference between: *InputStream classes* and *Outputstream classes*

InputStream classes	Outputstream classes
An input stream produces a stream of characters.	An output stream receives a stream of characters.

94. Difference between: *Yielding* and *Sleeping*

Yielding	Sleeping
It returns to the ready state.	It returns to the waiting state.

95. Difference between: *Thread's context class loader* and *Normal class loader*

Thread's context class loader	Normal classloader
It is the current class loader for the current thread.	Determines whether the class has been loaded previously. If so, return the previously loaded class.
An object can be created from a class in *ClassLoader* and then passed to a thread owned by *ClassLoader*. E.g., *Thread.currentThread(). getContextClass-Loader()*	Consult the Primordial Class Loader to attempt to load the class from the CLASSPATH. This prevents external classes from spoofing trusted Java classes. See whether the Class Loader is allowed to create the class being loaded. The Security Manager makes this decision. If not, throw a security exception. Read the class file into an array of bytes. The way this happens differs according to particular class loaders. Some class loaders may load classes from a local database. Others may load classes across the network. Construct a class object and its methods from the class file. Resolve classes immediately referenced by the class before it is used. These includes classes used by static initializers of the class and any classes that the class extends. Check the class file with the Verifier.

96. Difference between: *HashSet, TreeSet* and *LinkedHashSet*

HashSet	TreeSet	LinkedHashSet
Stores the elements in a hash table.	Stores elements in a red-black tree.	It is implemented as a hash table using linked list.
Sorting order is undefined.	Sorted in non descending order.	Uses insertion order.
Performance is better than *LinkedHashSet*.	Performance is slow.	It can add to the start of the list very fast. Also, it can delete fast from the interior using iteration.
Operations : *add, clear, clone, contains, isEmpty, iterat-or, remove* and *size*.	Operations: *add, addAll, ceiling, clear, clone, comparator, contains, descendingIterator, descendingSet, first, floor, hashSet, higher, isEmpty, iterator, last, lower, pollFirst, remove, size, subSet* and *tailSet*.	Operations: *add, clear, clone, contains, isEmpty, iterator, remove* and *size*.
`public class HashSet extends AbstractSet implements Set, Cloneable, Serializable {...}`	`public class TreeSet extends AbstractSet implements SortedSet, Cloneable, Serializable {...}`	`public class LinkedHashSet extends HashSet implements Set, Cloneable, Serializable {...}`

Similarities between:*HashSet, TreeSet* and *LinkedHashSet*
a. Stores unique values

97. Difference between: *ArrayList, Vector* and *LinkedList*

ArrayList	Vector	LinkedList
Resizable Array, unordered, allows duplicates and accepts null values.	Growable array of objects, unordered, allows duplicates and accepts null values. It can grow or shrink as needed.	Implemented similar to doubly-linked chain of nodes, unordered, allows duplicates and accepts null values.
Not synchronized. Hence not thread-safe. Use *ArrayList* if there is single thread.	Synchronized and thread-safe. Use *Vector* class when there are multiple threads in the system.	Not synchronized. Inserts at the beginning or end is very fast. Also, deletions from the middle is very fast.

Provides random access.	Provides random access.	Provides optimal sequential access.
public class ArrayList <E> extends AbstractList <E> implements List <E>, RandomAccess, Cloneable, Serializable	public class Vector <E> extends AbstractList <E> implements List <E>, RandomAccess ,Cloneable, Serializable	public class LinkedList <E> extends AbstractSequential− List <E> implements List <E>, Deque<E>, Cloneable, Serializable

98. Difference between: >> *operator* and >>> *operator*

>> operator	>>> operator
Arithmetic shift. Sign bit is preserved while shifting right.	Logical shift. Zeros are shifted in to replace the discarded bits.
Operator moves the bits towards right. It doesn't move the sign bit.	Operator moves the bits towards right with sign bit.

Similarities between:>> *operator* and >>> *operator*
a. Both operators shift from bits from most significant bit (MSB) side towards least significant bit (LSB).
b. Zeros are appended towards MSB side of number.

99. Difference between: *Class* and *Object*

Class	Object
A class is a template. It will have methods and fields.	An object is an instance of a class.
Class is a blue print of an object, which is a non-live entity.	Object is a live entity.

100. Difference between: *Instance, Object, Reference* and *Class*

Instance	Object	Reference	Class
Provides the values of data members of a class at a particular time.	An object is instance of a class.	A reference is similar to a pointer pointing to an object.	A class is a user defined data type with set of data members and member functions.

101. Difference between: *Object* and *Instance*

Object	Instance
An object may not have a class definition.	An instance will have class definition. Example: Employee emp=new Employee ();

102. Difference between: **= and ==**

=	==
Assignment operator.	Equality operator.
Used to assign a value to a variable.	Used to evaluate a logical condition whether it is equal or not.
int a=10;	if(a==b){}

103. Difference between: *JDBC and ODBC*

JDBC	ODBC
JDBC is for Java applications.	ODBC is for Microsoft applications.
JDBC API is a natural Java interface and is built on ODBC. JDBC has some of the basic features of ODBC.	ODBC cannot be used directly with Java because it uses a C interface. ODBC makes use of pointers, which are not supported by Java.
It is simple interface while allowing advanced capabilities.	Complex options for simple queries.
JDBC drivers are coded using Java, so JDBC code is automatically installable, secure and portable on all platforms.	ODBC requires manual installation of the ODBC driver manager and driver on all client machines.

104. Difference between: *Append* and *Concatenation*

Append	Concatenation
Used with *StringBuffer* to append character sequence or string.	Add a string at the end of another string.
This operation will not create a new object, rather it updates the object.	When we concatenate a string with another string, a new string object is created.

Example:	
StringBuffer buff = new StringBuffer(10); buff.append("Buffer ");	String str1 = "ABC"; String str2 = "123"; String com = str1.concat(str2);

Similarities between:*Append* **and** *Concatenation*
Both operations will merge string values.

105. Difference between: *Readers* **and** *Streams*

Readers	Streams
Character oriented.	Byte oriented.
It will support Unicode data.	Does not support Unicode data.

106. Difference between: *Lightweight component* **and** *Heavyweight component*

Lightweight component	Heavyweight component
Does not use native calls to obtain the graphical units.	For every call, there will be a native call to get the graphical units.
Lightweight components reuse its parent's graphical units.	Heavyweight components use native graphical unit for every component.
Lightweight components are faster.	Heavyweight components are slow.
Example: Swing	Example: AWT

107. Difference between: *Static class loader* **and** *Dynamic class loader*

Static class loader	Dynamic class loader
Static class loading happens as soon as Java compiler encounter the name of the class and the full name is placed in the class file. The JVM will use the name in the class file to load the class before its use.	Dynamic class loading happens when the code requests the JVM to load a class by using the class name as a *String* during execution. So, Java program can load the class on the fly.
Performed during compile time.	Performed during Run time / execution time.
Preloaded class.	Loading on request.

Example:	Example:
`ArrayList lst = new ArrayList(6);`	`Class clz = Class.forName( java.util.HashSet);`
Uses *new* operator.	Uses *Class.forName()* method.

108. Difference between: *Arguments* **and** *Parameters*

Arguments	Parameters
Arguments are the actual values that are passed when the method is invoked.	Parameters refer to the list of variables in a method declaration.
When you invoke a method, the arguments used must match the declaration's parameters by type and order.	Arguments and parameters are tightly coupled with data type.

Example:
 	
`int i = 3;`
`//invoke Method()`
`//with i as argument`
`Method(i);`
	Example:
	
	`// parameter in Method()`
	`public void Method(int a) {`
	`        a = 10;`
	`}`

109. Difference between: *Instantiation* **and** *Initialization*

Instantiation	Initialization
Creating an object.	Initializing the object.
The *new* keyword is used to create an object.	The *new* operator is followed by a call to a constructor which initializes the new object.
Example: `Area a = new Area ();`	Example: `Area a = new Area (12,15);`

110. Difference between: *Static nested classes* **and** *Non-static nested classes*

Static nested classes	Non-static nested classes

Inner classes that are declared static.	Inner classes which are not declared static.
Interacts with the instance members of its outer class. Static nested classes do not have access to other members of the enclosing class.	Inner class is associated with an instance of its enclosing class and has access to that object's methods and fields (even if they are declared private).

Example:
 	
`class A {`
  `...`
    `static class B {`
      `...`
    `}`
`}`
	Example:
	
	`class A {`
	  `...`
	    `class B{`
	      `...`
	    `}`
	`}`

111. Difference between: *Static enumerated type* and *Dynamic enumerated type*

Static enumerated type	Dynamic enumerated type
The set of possible values are fixed and does not vary during run time.	The possible values can increase or decrease at run time.
Example: Week days (7 days are fixed).	Example: Car models (models could change every year).

112. Difference between: *Class Methods* and *Instance Methods*

Class Methods	Instance Methods
These are static methods.	Instance methods are not declared as static.
Operate on class members and not on instance members as class methods are unaware of instance members.	Instance methods of the class can also not be called from within a class method. Instance methods operate on specific instances of classes.
The method can be called without creating an instance of the class.	This method requires an instance of the class to exist before they can be called. So an instance of a class needs to be created by using the *new* keyword.

113. Difference between: *Enumeration* and *Iterator*

Enumeration	Iterator
It doesn't have *remove()* method.	It has *remove()* method.
Enumeration acts as read-only interface, because it has the methods only to traverse and fetch the objects.	Can be *abstract, final, native, static* or *synchronized*.

114. Difference between: *Reflection* and *Introspection*

Reflection	Introspection
Reflection is the ability to examine or alter the runtime behaviour of applications running in the JVM. Reflection is a powerful technique and can enable programs to perform operations which would otherwise be not possible.	Introspection is the automatic analysing process a bean's design patterns to reveal the bean's events, properties and methods. This process controls the publishing and discovery of bean operations and properties.
We can reflect any class that we load but with a certain extent to the constraints of any security manager that is applied. We can load any class if you can get the byte-code for it and its direct and indirect dependencies.	The relationship between Introspection and Reflection can be seen as similar to JavaBeans and other Java classes.

115. Difference between: *Shallow copy* and *Deep copy*

Shallow copy	Deep copy
Values of the pointers/references are copied.	Copies everything including referenced objects.
Shallow copy of a collection is copy of the collection structure only, but not the elements. By this action, two collections share the same elements. Hence, redundancy is avoided.	Deep copy duplicates everything which is referenced. A deep copy of a collection will result into two collections of elements in original collection.
Example: Object *A* points to object *B* location in memory.	Example: All elements in object *B*'s memory location is copied to object *A*'s memory location.

116. Difference between: *Up casting* and *Down casting*

Up casting	Down casting

Used to treat an object of a subclass type as an object of super class type.	Used to treat an object of a super class type to be treated as an object of subclass type.
This is implicit process of converting the subclass reference to a super class reference without using the cast operation.	A super class reference can be converted into a subclass reference, but this casted subclass reference cannot call the methods of super classes.
Casting up the inheritance tree to a more general type.	Casting down the inheritance tree to a more specific class. In other words, casting a super class to subclass.

117. Difference between: *Runtime polymorphism* **and** *Compile time polymorphism*

Runtime polymorphism	Compile time polymorphism
Method call is resolved at run time.	Method call is resolved at compile time.
JVM decides where to jump to execute the method body while running the program.	Compiler decides in advance where to jump to execute the method body.
It is slower than runtime.	It is faster than runtime, but the size of compiled code might be high.
Dynamic / late binding.	Static / early binding.
Example: Method overriding using inheritance.	Example: Method Overloading.

118. Difference between: *Method overriding through inheritance* **and** *Method overriding through interface*

Method overriding through inheritance	Method overriding through interface
Uses *extends* keyword.	Uses *interface* keyword.

Example:

```java
public class A {
        String name;
                public A() {
                }
public A(String nam) {
                name = nam;
                }
public String getName() {
return "Name:"+name ;
}


}
public class B extends A {
        int age;
public B(String nam, int a){
                name = nam;
                age = a;
                }

public String getName(){
return    "Name:"+name
 +",Age:"+age;
        }
}
public class Test{
public static void
main(String[] args) {
A a = new A("Vaishu");
B b = new B("Bhavana", 26);
System.out.println(
a.getName());
System.out.println(
b.getName());
}
}
```

Output:
Name: Vaishu
Name: Bhavana , Age:26

Example:

```java
public interface A {
        public void method();
}
public interface B
extends A {
        public void method();
}
public class Test
implements B{
public void method() {
System.out.println("Hi");
}
        public static void
        main(String[] args) {
        Test t =new Test();
        t.method();
        }
}
```

Output:
Hi

119. Difference between: *Stub* and *Skeleton*

Stub	Skeleton
This is a proxy for a remote object that runs on the client system.	This is a proxy for a remote object that runs on the server system.

Stub is used to present the same interfaces as the remote server. Remote method calls initiated by the client are actually directed to the stub.	Skeleton is used to dispatch the call to the actual remote object implementation.
Steps involved in communication, 1. Initiates a connection with the remote JVM containing the remote object. 2. Marshals the parameters to the remote JVM. 3. Waits for the result of the method invocation. 4. Unmarshals the return value or exception returned and returns the value to the caller.	Steps involved in communication, 1.Unmarshals the parameters for the remote method. 2.Invokes the method on the actual object. 3. Marshals the result to the caller.

120. Difference between: *Pre increment* and *Post increment*

Pre increment	Post increment
++ Prefix varibale	Postfix variable ++
Performs the increment operation and returns the value of the increment operation.	Returns the current value of entire expression and then performs the increment operation on that value.
Example: int a = 0; ++a;	Example: int a = 0; a++;

121. Difference between: *Labelled break statement* and *Unlabelled break statement*

Labelled *break* statement	Unlabelled *break* statement
It terminates and transferes the control to the statement following label.	It terminates the innermost *switch, for, while,* or *do-while* loop / block.

Example:
 	
``
Label:
for(i=0;i<arr.length;i++){
for(j=0;j<arr[i].length;j++){
if (arr[i][j] == searchfor){
    break Label;
        }
    }
}
``
	Example:
	
	``
	for(i=0;i<arr.length;i++) {
	for(j=0;j<arr[i].length;j++){
	if (arr[i][j] == searchfor){
	            break;
	        }
	    }
	}
	``

122. Difference between: *File and Random access file*

File	Random access file
It encapsulates the files and directories of the local file system.	It provides methods to read and write the data to the file.

123. Difference between: *length and length()*

length	length()
The *length* field is used to find out the array length/size.	The *length()* method is used to find out the *String* length.
| Example:<br><br>```
String s[]={new String("AB"),
new String("CD")};


int j=s.length;
System.out.println("j="+j);
``` | Example:<br><br>```
String str=new String("AB");
int i=str.length();
System.out.println("i="+i);
``` |

124. Difference between: *Programming language, Scripting language and Markup language*

Programming language	Scripting language	Markup language
Program should be compiled before it is executed.	Script is interpreted at run-time.	It is a set of tags that are used to "mark up" text documents and they are logically arranged and labelled.
Typed, compiled and interpreted.	Dynamically typed and interpreted.	Browser parses the document and displays the data as per the tags.
Example: C, C++, VB, Java etc	Example: PHP, ASP, JSP, JavaScript, VBScript etc	Example: HTML, XML etc

125. Difference between: *Coupling and Cohesion*

Coupling	Cohesion
One object interacts with another object. There could be unnecessary dependence of one component upon another component's implementation.	A certain class performs a set of closely related actions. Basically components interact with each other semantically.

Strong coupling is less flexible and less scalable.	Difficulty to manage when more and more behaviours become scattered.
How class is closely integrated with implementations of other classes, that a change in any other class will result in change in this class.	Cohesion is closely related to the various functions of a class.

126. Difference between: *JAVA and J2EE*

JAVA	J2EE
It is a programming language.	It is a platform and it is a implementation of the Java programming language.
Generally, it is used for business application, internet programming, games, etc.	Generally, it is used for business organizations, enterprise applications and distributed applications, web applications etc.

127. Difference between: *Tomcat server and Web logic server*

Tomcat server	Web logic server
It is a web-server.	It is an application-server.
It is a 3-tier architecture.	It is N-tier Architecture.
It only runs servlets, JSP etc. but we cannot deploy an EJB.	We can deploy an EJB along with servlets and JSPs.
Handles only HTTP protocol.	Handles FTP and HTTP.

128. Difference between: *JRE and JAR*

JRE	JAR
Java Runtime Environment.	Java ARchive.
It includes Java Virtual Machine and some other library files.	It contains the classes, images, sound files, help files, etc for a Java application.
It does not contain any development tools such as compiler, debugger, etc.	It is in ZIP file format.
It runs a Java application.	It is used to distribute Java applications or libraries, in the form of classes and associated metadata and resources.

129. Difference between: **C++ and *Java***

Feature	C++	Java
Pointers	Supported	Not Supported.
Preprocessor	Supported	Does not support.
Operator loading	Supported	Does not support.
Compilation	Compiled	Compiled and interpreted.
Multiple inheritance	Supported	Can achieve through interface.
structures or unions	Includes	Not supported
Global variables	Supported	Not Supported, but you can achieve similar thing using *static* variables.
Header files	It has header files	It does not have header files. Packages can be imported.
Automatic type conversion	Supported	Does not perform automatically
Destructors	Allowed	Not allowed. However, destruction can be achieved using *finalize*() function.
Delete operator	*delete* operator is provided	Does not provide *delete* operator.
Templates	Supported	Does not support.
Default member access	Package level access (more public)	Private.
Portability	Not fully portable.	Yes and platform-independent
Speed	Faster compare to Java.	Slow because of 2 steps to run a application (compile and interpret)
Pass by value and pass by reference	Both Supported	Supports pass by value
Common root object	Not achievable	Java has a common root object for all objects
Built in exception class hierarchy	Not available	Java has a built in exception class hierarchy
Runtime polymorphism	Not supported	Supported
Primitive data type	*bool, char, float, double, int, long int, short int, unsigned int, unsigned long int* and *unsigned short int*	*byte, short, char, int, long, float, double* and *boolean*

Typedefs and defines	Available	Not available
System dependent	Yes	No
Automatic garbage collection	No	Yes

Similarities between:**C++ and** *Java*
a) Function Overloading
b) Function Overriding
c) break, continue statements
d) Loops
e) Constructors.
f) Polymorphism is achieved by method overloading and method overriding.
g) int,char,long, short,float and double.
i) Few keywords.

130. Overview Comparison of C++, JAVA and PHP

Features	C++	Java	PHP
Pointers	Supported	Not Supported	Supported references
Preprocessor	Supported	Not Supported	Implicitly does it, processes the code before execution or compilation.
Operator overloading	Supported	Not Supported	Limited
Compiled and/or Interpreted	Compiled	Compiled and interpreted	Interpreted
Multiple inheritance	Supported	Can achieve through interface	Can be achieved
Structures or unions	Included	Not Supported	Not Supported
Annotations	Supported	Supported	Supported
Global variables	Supported	Not Supported, but can be achieve using static variable.	Supported, *GLOBAL* keyword can be used.
Header files	It has header files	It does not have but have *import* to including packages.	The *include* statement includes and evaluates the specified file.
Automatic type conversion	Supported	Not supported	Supported
Constructors	Allowed	Allowed	Allowed

Destructors	Allowed	It does not allow, instead similar thing can be achieved using *finalize*().	It is allowed using _*destruct*().
The *delete* operator	Provides *delete* operator.	Not provided	Does not have *delete* operator.
Templates	Supported	Does not support.	Does not support.
Default member access	Package level access (more *public*).	*private*	*public*
Portability	Not fully portable	Yes, it is platform-independent.	Yes, it is platform-independent.
Speed	Faster compared to JAVA.	Slow in comparison to C++.	Slow compared to C++.
Pass by value and pass by reference.	Both Supported.	Pass by value is supported.	Pass by value is supported.
Common root object	Not supported	Java has a common root object for all objects	Not achievable
Built in exception class hierarchy	Not available	Available	Available
Runtime polymorphism	Not Supported	Supported	Supported
System dependent	Yes	No	No
Supporting object serialization	Serializes to a stream.	Serializes to a stream or to XML	Serializes to a stream.
Interfaces	Not supported	Supported	Not supported
Scope of class members	*public*, *protected*, and *private*	*public*, *private*, *protected* and default (package)	Only default public scope
Security	Yes	Yes	Yes
Multithreading	No	Yes	Yes
Automatic garbage collection	No	Yes	Yes
Function overloading	Yes	Yes	No
Function overriding	Yes	Yes	Yes
break and *continue*	Yes	Yes	Yes
Loops	Yes	Yes	Yes
Destructors	Yes	No	Yes
Few data types are common	Yes	Yes	Yes
Method overloading	Supported	Supported	Supported
Abstract classes and methods	Supported	Supported	Supported

Exception handling	Achieved through *try, catch* and *throw*	Achieved through *try,catch, throw* and *finally*.	Achieved through *try, catch* and *throw*

131. Language Architecture

C++ Language Architecture	Java Language Architecture	PHP Language Architecture
| ```
+-------------------+
|   Source Code     |
| (e.g., hello.cpp) |
|                   |
+-------------------+

         ⇓

+-------------------+
|                   |
|   Compiler        |
+-------------------+

         ⇓

+-------------------+
|                   |
|  Object Code      |
| (e.g., hello.obj) |
+-------------------+

         ⇓

+-------------------+
|                   |
|   Linker          |
+-------------------+

         ⇓

+-------------------+
|                   |
|  Machine code     |
+-------------------+

         ⇓

+-------------------+
|       OS          |
|   +-----------+   |
|   |  CPU      |   |
|   +-----------+   |
+-------------------+
``` | ```
+-------------------+
|    Source Code    |
| (e.g., Hello.java)|
|                   |
+-------------------+

         ⇓

+-------------------+
|                   |
|Java Compiler(JIT) |
+-------------------+

         ⇓

+-------------------+
|                   |
|   Byte Code       |
| (e.g., Hello.class)|
+-------------------+

         ⇓

+-------------------+
|Java Virtual Machine|
| +---------------+ |
| |      OS       | |
| | +-----------+ | |
| | |  CPU      | | |
| | +-----------+ | |
| +---------------+ |
+-------------------+
``` | ```
+-------------------+
|   Source Code     |
| (e.g., hello.php) |
|                   |
+-------------------+

         ⇓

+-------------------+
|  Opcode           |
|  Compiler(Zend)   |
+-------------------+

         ⇓

+-------------------+
|                   |
| Opcode Optimizer  |
| Opcode Cache      |
+-------------------+

         ⇓

+-------------------+
|                   |
| Opcode Executor   |
+-------------------+

         ⇓

+-------------------+
|       OS          |
|   +-----------+   |
|   |  CPU      |   |
|   +-----------+   |
+-------------------+
``` |

132. Program Structure in C++, JAVA and PHP
```

Structure of C++ Language	Structure of Java Language	Structure of PHP Language
| ```
+--------------------+
|   Header file      |
|   Declaration      |
+--------------------+

          ⇓

+--------------------+
|   Global           |
|   Declaration      |
+--------------------+

          ⇓

+--------------------+
| Class Declaration  |
| and Method         |
| Definition         |
+--------------------+

          ⇓

+--------------------+
|   Main function    |
+--------------------+

          ⇓

+--------------------+
|   Method           |
|   Definition       |
+--------------------+
``` | ```
+--------------------+
| Documentation      |
| Section(suggest)   |
+--------------------+

          ⇓

+--------------------+
| Package Statement  |
| (optional)         |
+--------------------+

          ⇓

+--------------------+
| Import Statements  |
|(optional)          |
+--------------------+

          ⇓

+----------------------+
| Interface Statements |
| (optional)           |
+----------------------+

          ⇓

+----------------------+
| Class Definitions    |
| (optional)           |
+----------------------+

          ⇓

+----------------------+
| Main Method          |
| (Mandatory)          |
+----------------------+
``` | ```
+--------------------+
|   Includes Code    |
+--------------------+

          ⇓

+--------------------+
| Define Globals     |
+--------------------+

          ⇓

+--------------------+
| Helper functions   |
+--------------------+

          ⇓

+--------------------+
| Main script logic  |
+--------------------+
``` |
```

133. Sample Program in C++, JAVA and PHP

C++	Java	PHP

Program Name:
HelloWorld.cpp
#include <iostream.h>
int main ()
{
  cout << "Hello World!";
  return 0;
}
	Program Name:
	HelloWorld.java
	public class HelloWorld {
	public static void main
	(String[] args)
	{
	System.out.
	println("Hello World!");
	}
	}
		Program Name:
		HelloWorld.php
		<?php
		 echo "Hello World!";
		?>

Chapter 3

Java Programs

Find the output of below programs.

```
1. class T {
        int i=20;
        T(){
                this(i++);
        }

        T(int i){
                this.i=i;
        }

        public static void main (String[] args){
                new T();
        }
}
```

Output: T.java:4: error: cannot reference *i* before supertype constructor has been called this(*i* + +);

Explanation: Cannot refer to an instance field *i* while explicitly invoking a constructor because *i* is an instance variable of the class *T*, that means, when an object of type *T* is created, a unique instance of *i* is also created and attached to that particular object of *T*. Since this case, it is impossible to reference *i* in the constructor as neither it nor the object have been created so far. To come out such issues, make a variable static which becomes associated with the class *T* itself rather than instances of that class and it is also shared amongst all instances of a class *T*. This is because, normally static variables are created when the JVM first loads the class. When we use *T* to create an instance the class, by this time class is already loaded and the static variable is ready to use including the constructor. Hence no error/exception is thrown. Below updated program compiles without an error.
Example:

```
class T {
static int i=20;
T(){
this(i++);
}
```

```
T(int i){
this.i=i;
}
public static void main (String[] args){
new T();
}
}
```

2. ```
class T {
int i;
        public static void main(String argv[]) {
                int j= new T().i;
                System.out.println(j+","+new T().i);

        }
}
```
Output:
0,0

Explanation: Usually all member variables are initialized during creation of the object. Default value of variables and its type is given in the below table,

| Variable Type | Default Value |
|---|---|
| byte | 0 |
| short | 0 |
| int | 0 |
| long | 0L |
| float | 0f |
| double | 0d |
| char | *null* |
| boolean | false |
| reference | *null* |

3. ```
class T
{
public static void main(String argv[])
{
int i[]={111,222};
int j[]=(int[])i.clone();
System.out.println((i==j)? "A":"B");
i[1]++;
```

```
System.out.println(j[1]);
    }
}
Output:
        B
    222
```

Explanation:

The *clone()* function creates a new object with a copy of the original object. While invoking a *clone* method on an array, it returns a reference to a new array which includes (or references) the same elements as the source array.

As shown in above example, *int i[]* and *int j[]* both are separate object instances created on the heap, note here, array *i* and *j* are objects but elements are non-objects. If we alter *int j[]*, the changes would not be reflected on *int i[]* as these two arrays are separate object instances.

What happens if source array contains objects? The clone method will return a reference to a new array, but that references the same objects as the source array. See below example:

```
class Test{
    private String name;
    public Test(String name) {
        super();
        this.name = name;
    }

    public String getName() {
        return name;
    }
    public void setName(String name) {
        this.name = name;
    }
}
```

and we create and populate an array of type Test,

```
Test[] testArr = new Test[4];
testArr[0] = new Test("T1");
testArr[1] = new Test("T2");
testArr[2] = new Test("T3");
testArr[3] = new Test("T4");
```

then clone the testArr,

```
Test[] testArrClone = testArr.clone();
```

the arrays refer to the same elements.

```
System.out.println(testArr[0] == testArrClone[0]
? "Same":"Different");
System.out.println(testArr[1] == testArrClone[1]
? "Same":"Different");
System.out.println(testArr[2] == testArrClone[2]
? "Same":"Different");
System.out.println(testArr[3] == testArrClone[3]
? "Same":"Different");
```

All above 4 outputs will print "Same" 4 times. This means that if we alter an object accessed via cloned array, the changes will be reflected when we access the same object in the source array, because they associate the same reference.

```
testArrClone[0].setName("ABC");
System.out.println(testArr[0].getName());
```

This prints "ABC". However, changes to the array itself will only affect that array.

```
testArrClone[1] = new Test("DEF");
System.out.println(testArrClone[1].getName());
System.out.println(testArr[1].getName());
```

This outputs "DEF" and "T2".

4.
```
import java.util.StringTokenizer;
class TEST        {
        public static void main(String argv[])   {
                String str="1 2 1.2  3.4 5  6";
                StringTokenizer tokens= new StringTokenizer(str);
                while(tokens.hasMoreElements())
                System.out.println(tokens.nextToken());
        }
}
```

Output:
1
2
1.2
3.4
5
6

Explanation: *StringTokenizer(String str)* constructs a string tokenizer for the specified string. The tokenizer uses the following default delimiters \t \ n \ r and \f which corresponds to space or tab character, newline character, carriage-return character and form-feed character respectively. Delimiter characters themselves will not be treated as tokens.

5.
```
class TEST        {
        public static void main(String argv[])   {
                String str;
                str="123456";
                int j=Integer.valueOf(str).intValue();
                System.out.println(j);
                str="123.456";
```

```
                  double  d=Double.valueOf(str).doubleValue();
                  System.out.println(d);
            }
}
```

Output:
```
      123456
      123.456
```

Explanation: *Integer.valueOf (String str)* returns an *Integer* object corresponding to the integer value of *String* argument. The argument is interpreted as representing a signed decimal integer, similar to argument provided to *parseInt(java.lang.String)* method. Similarly, *Double.valueOf(String str)* returns a *Double* object holding the double value represented by the string *str* argument.

6.
```
class  TEST        {
       public  static  void  main(String[]  args)  {
                int  j  =  fun();
       }

       public  int  fun()             {
                return  1;
       }
}
```

Output: Compiler Error:cannot make a static reference to the non static method *fun()* from the TEST.
Explanation:
Always static method(*main()*) belongs to a class, but non static methods belongs to the object of the class. Let us explain more on this statement. When you call *fun()* from *main*, you get an error because main is not associated with any object/instance. In the above program, it is clear that *fun()* is non-static you cannot call from a *static* method. A class instance (non-static) methods work on objects that are of a particular class type. These are created with the keyword new like below code:

```
Test  myTest  =  new  Test();
```

To call an instance method, you can call it on a instance (*myTest*): *myTest.fun()* We can also call a static fields/methods with an object reference like *myTest.staticMethod()* but this is strongly discouraged because it does not make it clear that they are class variables. See below example, here static variable will have single value for instance as well as for entire class.

```
class  Test  {
String  text  =  "100";
String  fun()  {  return  text;  }
static  String  SIZE  =  "123";
public  static  void  main(String[]  args)  {
Test  t1  =  new  Test();
t1.text  =  "500";
System.out.println("t1.text="+  t1.text);
System.out.println("t1.SIZE="+  t1.SIZE);
System.out.println("SIZE="+  SIZE);
```

```
Test  t2  =  new  Test ();
Test.SIZE  =  "111";
System.out.println("t2.text="+ t2.text);
System.out.println("t2.SIZE="+ t2.SIZE);
System.out.println("SIZE="+ SIZE);
}
}
Output:
t1.text=500
t1.SIZE=123
SIZE=123
t2.text=100
t2.SIZE=111
SIZE=111
```

Static method can call only *static* methods or *static* methods can only access *static* data members or fields. The *static* methods cannot refer this and *super*. A *static* method is always invoked with/without reference to a particular object. We may not notice a error if you try to invoke *static* method using the keyword *this* or the keyword *super*. A Java *static* method cannot access instance variables directly.

```
Solution  to  above  program:
class  TEST
{
        public  static  void  main(String[]  args)  {
                TEST  t=new  TEST();
                int  i=t.fun();
        }
        public  int  fun()              {
                return  1;
        }
}
```

7.

```
class  TEST          {
        public  static  void  main(String[]  args) {
                String  str1  =  new  String("ABCD");
                String  str2  =  new  String("ABCD");
                if  (str1  ==  str2)
                        System.out.println("SAME");
                else
                        System.out.println("DIFFERENT");
        }
}

output:
DIFFERENT
```

Explanation: == tests whether both objects are same. However it does not tests whether the values of both objects are same. The == checks for reference equality and .equals() checks for value equality. Therefore, if you really want to check whether two strings have the same value, then you should use .equals(). In some cases yet where we can guarantee that two strings with the same value will be represented by the same object because of String interning. See below table where different possibilities are shown.

Action	Code	Result
Strings have the same value	new String("test").equals("test")	true
String Object v/s String	new String("test") = = "test"	false
Both are String Objects	new String("test") = = new String("test")	false
Literal v/s literal: interned by the compiler and hence refer to the same object	"test" == "test"	true
Compile time concatenation of string literals	"test" == "te" + "st"	true
At runtime, substring() is invoked which is generating distinct objects	"test" == "!test".substring(1)	false
Recalling interned strings using .intern()	"test" == "!test".substring(1).intern()	true

String interning is a process of storing only one copy of each distinct string value, which must be immutable which makes some string processing tasks more time or space-efficient at the cost of involving more time when the string is created or interned. Generally distinct values are stored in a string intern pool. The 'intern' is a single copy of each string and it is generally looked up by a method String.intern(), all compile-time constant strings are automatically interned using this method.

The == is a bit cheaper than equals() (a single reference comparison saves time compare to a method call), hence, in some circumstances where it is guarantee that you are dealing with only interned strings, then == is better for performance improvement.

```
class TEST {
        public static void main(String[] args) {
                String str1 = "ABCD";
                String str2 = "ABCD";
                if (str1 == str2)
                        System.out.println("SAME");
                else
                        System.out.println("DIFFERENT");
        }
}

output:
SAME
```

Explanation: As explained in the previous problem, both the strings are literals. Both literals are referring to the same object. Hence the output.

8.

9.
```java
class TEST {
        public static void main(String[] args) {
                String str1 = "ABC";
                String str2 = "ABCD";
                if (str1 == str2)
                        System.out.println("SAME");
                else
                        System.out.println("DIFFERENT");
        }
}
```

output:
DIFFERENT

Explanation: In this case, *str1* and *str2* are referring to the different object. Hence the output.

10.
```java
class TEST {
        public static int i;
        static   {
                i=1;
                System.out.println("STATIC");
        }
        public static void main(String[] args) {
        new TEST();
        System.out.println("main()");
        }
        TEST()   {
                System.out.println(" i = " + i);
        }
}
```

output:
STATIC
i = 1
main()

Explanation: *STATIC* will be printed first, because *static* blocks are executed before the *main()*.
A static initialization block is a like a regular block of code enclosed in braces   and preceded by the *static* keyword.
The *static* keyword works with variables, methods, blocks, nested class, etc. The static keyword belongs to the class than instance of the class. It can be used for memory management too. Static keyword can be used in the below cases,

(a) Static variable (class variable):

Static variables are declared in classes or methods with *static* modifier. Only one copy is stored in *static* memory associated to a class (class variables). It is created/initialized during class loading in memory.

Example:

```
class Student{
    int id;
    String name;
    // static variable declaration
    static String college ="ORACLE, Bangalore";

    Student(int i, String str){
    id = i;
    name = str;
    }
    void display (){
    System.out.println(id+" "+name+" "+college);
    }

    public static void main(String args[]){
    Student s1 = new Student(1001,"Chandrakant");
    s1.display();
    }
}
```

Output:

1001 Chandrakant ORACLE, Bangalore

(b) Static method (class method):

No need to instantiate a class (including abstract by extending etc.) in order to call a static method. Methods marked *static* belong to the class rather than to any particular instance of the class. Static methods can't be overridden. They can be redefined in a subclass (redefining and overriding are not the same thing). It is known as Hiding. A static method cannot access non-static/instance variables, because a static method is never associated with any instance. Static method can access non-static methods by using instances. By definition, a non-static method is one that is called on instance of some class, whereas a static method belongs to the class itself.

Example:

```
    class Student{
    static int id;
    static String name;
    static String college ="ORACLE, Bangalore";

    Student(int i, String str){
    id = i;
    name = str;
    }
    static void display (){
    System.out.println(id+" "+name+" "+college);
    }

    public static void main(String args[]){
```

```
    Student s1 = new Student(1001,"Chandrakant");
    display();
    }
    }
```

Output:
1001 Chandrakant ORACLE, Bangalore

(c) Static block:

Static block is a static initializer. Typically it is executed when the class is loaded. A static block is enclosed in braces { }, preceded with *static* keyword. If a class has multiple *static* blocks across the class, then JVM combines them as a single block of code and executes it.

Example:

```
class Student{
    static int id;
    static String name;
    static String college ="ORACLE, Bangalore";

    static{ // static block
    id=1002;
    name="Static Block";
    college="New College";
    System.out.println(id+" "+name+" "+college);
    }
    Student(int i,String str, String colz){
    id = i;
    name = str;
    college=colz;
    }
    void display (){
    System.out.println(id+" "+name+" "+college);
    }

    public static void main(String args[]){
    Student s1 = new Student(1001,"Chandrakant", "UVCE");
    s1.display();
    }
    }
```

Output:
1002 Static Block New College
1001 Chandrakant UVCE

(d) Static nested class(Static class):

A static class is created within a another class is called static nested class. As usual, it cannot access non-static data members and methods however it can be accessed by it's outer class name. This class can access static data members of outer class including *private*.

Example:

```
    class Student{
    static int id;
    static String name;
    static String college;
```

```
static class Inner { //static class
void display(){
id=1002;
name="Static Block";
college="New College";
System.out.println(id+" "+name+" "+college);
}
}
public static void main(String args[]){
Student.Inner in=new Student.Inner();
in.display();
}
}
```

Output:
1002 Static Block New College

(e) Static variables and multi-threading:

Static variable is one per class-loader, if you need a per-thread value, make a static *ThreadLocal<T>*. Static variable is a shared value among different threads. So, we require to make sure that the access to static variables in multi-threaded environment is synchronized. Generally every thread has its own stack but they share the process heap. Stack holds only the local variables and these are stored in the PermGen section of the heap and so access to them should be well guarded.

(f) Static import:

It is similar to standard import statement in Java, but it permits to import one or all static members of a class. By importing static method, you can call them like they are defined in same class, similarly by static importing fields, we can access them without mentioning the class name.

Example:

```
//Test Student
package com.p1.p2.p3.p4;
public class Student {
    public static final int ID = 1001;
    public static int IDNumber(int num){
       return num + ID;
    }
}

//Test class
import static com.p1.p2.p3.p4.Student.*; //static import
public class Test {
    public static void main(String a[]){
        System.out.println("ID value: "+ID);
        int count = 100;
        System.out.println("ID count: "+IDNumber(count));
    }
}
```

Output:
ID value: 1001
ID count: 1101

(g) final static variable:

We can assign a value either in constructor or with the declaration for non-static final variables. But, we cannot assign a value in the constructor for *static final* variables, that means, they must be assigned a value while declaring them.

Example:

```java
class Test {
    static final int SIZE = 100;
    public static void main(String args[]){
    System.out.println("SIZE="+SIZE);
    }
}
```

Output:
SIZE=100

(h) Private static v/s public static:

Public static or private static is similar to regular private/public depends on whether you want the variables to be visible outside the class or not. If *static* keyword used, it can be accessed as *ClassName.varName*, for *private static*, you only access it from inside the class where it is defined but public static can be accessed from outside of the class too. Typically, *public static* or *private static* variables are often used for constants.

Example:

```java
class Student {
//outside class cannot access
    private final static int ID = 1001;
//We can access from Outside/Inside
    public final static String  NAME="Chandrakant";
    public static void main(String[] args) {
    System.out.println("Student.ID="+Student.ID);
    System.out.println("Student.NAME="+Student.NAME);
    }
}
```

Output:
Student.ID=1001
Student.NAME=Chandrakant

(i) Synchronizing static method/variable:

Static methods are not inherited. The lock will be on the class not on object if we make any static method as synchronized. If we require to guard the static variable's access, just locking an object instance does not protect access to static variables automatically, since there may be more than one instances and all of them use the same static variables. Hence, we have to have a lock on the class. A synchronized static block can be used to protect access to the static variables, a lock on a static method has no impact on any instances of that class.

Static variables are not inherited, but can be accessed using class's name. Having a new static synchronized method in a derived class cannot protect other threads to access static variables defined in its parent class nor should you use synchronized(this.getClass()) which locks the actual class might be the derived class. Hence, an explicit block synchronization is preferred way.

Example:

```java
class Employee{
    synchronized static void getSalary(int n){
```

```
        for(int  i=1;i<=10;i++){
          System.out.println(n*i);
          try{
            Thread.sleep(400);
          }catch(Exception e){}
        }
      }
    }

    class Emp1 extends Thread{
    public void run(){
    Employee.getSalary(10000);
    }
    }

    class Emp2 extends Thread{
    public void run(){
    Employee.getSalary(20000);
    }
    }

  public class Test{
    public static void main(String t[]){
    Emp1 e1=new Emp1();
    Emp2 e2=new Emp2();
    e1.start();
    e2.start();
    }
    }
Output:
10000
20000
30000
.
.
```

(j) Static array:
In static array allocation, some size has been predetermined, may be at compile time. Arrays objects are always allocated at runtime not necessarily it is dynamic, a dynamic array may be still a static, that is, it can't be changed at runtime. Hence, a concrete instance of array can not be resized ever once created.
Example:

```
public class Test  {
  static Integer[] ARR;
  static {
    ARR = new Integer[] { new Integer(100),
        new Integer(200), new Integer(300) };
  }

  public static void main(String args[]) {
```

```
      for (int i = 0; i < ARR.length; i++) {
        System.out.println(ARR[i]);
      }
    }
  }
```
Output:
100
200
300

(k) Static interface :
The static modifier is permitted on a nested classes or interfaces. In Java, Entry is nested inside the Map interface. For interfaces, the static modifier is actually optional. Because, it makes no sense for interfaces since they have no code.
Example:

```
interface Interf
{
  interface NestInterf1 {
  void fun1();
  }
  public static interface NestInterf2 {
  void fun2();
  }
}

public class InterfaceDemo implements Interf.NestInterf1,
Interf.NestInterf2
{
  public void fun1()
  {
    System.out.println("within from fun1");
  }

  public void fun2()
  {
    System.out.println("within from fun2");
  }
  public static void main (String args[])
  {
    Interf.NestInterf1 i1 = new InterfaceDemo();
    i1.fun1();
    Interf.NestInterf2 i2 = (Interf.NestInterf2) i2;
    i2.fun2();
  }
}
```
Output:
within from fun1
within from fun2

(l) Static methods in interfaces:

In Java 8(not older versions), interfaces can have static methods, and also we can override static methods with a default implementation.

(m) Static Map:

This is similar to static array.

Example:

```
import java.util.HashMap;
import java.util.Map;
class MapTest {
    private static final Map mp=new HashMap();
    static {
        mp.put(1, "Chandrakant");
        mp.put(2, "Vaishnavi");
                mp.put(3, "Bangalore");
    }
        public static void main (String args[])
        {
          System.out.println(mp);
        }
}
```

Output:

{1=Chandrakant, 2=Vaishnavi, 3=Bangalore}

Similarly, Static StringBuffer and static StringBuilder works.

(n) Static objects:

A static object is typically used for encapsulation of data and related functions. A static object need not have to have a *main* function.

Example:

```
class Test {
    String s;
    private static Test sc;

    static {
        sc = new Test();
    }

        public static void main (String[] args)
         throws java.lang.Exception
        {
        sc.s = "Chandrakant";
        System.out.println(sc.s);
        }
}
```

Output:

Chandrakant

11.
```java
class TEST {
        public static int i;
        {
                i = 1;
                System.out.println("BLOCK");
        }
        public static void main(String[] args) {
                new TEST();
                System.out.println("main()");
        }
        TEST()  {
                System.out.println(" i = " + i);
        }
}
```

output:
BLOCK
i = 1
main()

Explanation: Static block is executed before *main*() block.

12.
```java
public class TEST {
        static   int f() {
                System.out.println("f()");
                return 1;
        }
        public static void main(String[] args) {
                TEST c=new TEST();
                TEST.f();
                c.f();
        }
}
```

output:
f()
f()

Explanation: *static* members can be accessed through instance or through class name itself.

13.
```java
public class TEST {
        public static void main(String[] args) {
                System.out.println("hi".replace('i', 'h'));
        }
}
```

output:
hh

Explanation: Replaces *i* character by *h*. *replace(oldChar, newChar)* method returns a new string resulting from replacing all occurrences of *oldChar* in a string with *newChar*.
Consider below example where it prints "hi".

```
class TEST {
        public static void main(String[] args) {
                String s="hi";
                s.replace('i', 'h');
                System.out.println(s);
        }
}
Output:
hi
```

This is because, basically Strings in Java are immutable. It means that, when *replace* called, it does not change the contents of the existing string but it returns a new string with the modifications. Hence, *s.replace('i', 'h');* does not alter *s*. This technique is applicable to all the methods in the *String* class like *substring, toLowerCase*, etc.

14.
```
public class TEST {
        TEST  TEST()     {
                System.out.println("hi");
                TEST t=null;
                return t;
        }
        public static void main(String[] args) {
                TEST t= new TEST();
        }
}
Output:
Does not print anything
```

Explanation: Constructors does not return any value. Hence *TEST TEST()...* is considered as normal method instead of a constructor. This method has to be called explicitly. However default constructor is executed during object creation. The compiler automatically creates a no-argument constructor if no specific constructor is explicitly defined.

15.
```
public class Test{
        private static int i=0;
        Test()  {
                this.i = 1000;
```

```
        }
        public static void main(String[] args) {
            i = 1;
                Test t= new Test();
                System.out.println(i);
                System.out.println(t.i);
                int i=2;
                Test t1= new Test();
                System.out.println(i);
                System.out.println(t1.i);
        }
}
```

Output:
1000
1000
2
1000

Explanation: Local variable will have high priority. Instance variables are hidden not overridden. When a local variable have the same name as one of the instance variable, the local variable shadows the instance variable within the method block.

16.
```
public class Test        {
        public static void main(String[] args) {
        int arr[]=new int[3];
        arr[1]+= arr[1]+=-arr[1]-(-10);
        System.out.println(arr[1]);
        }
}
```
Output:10

Explanation: Expression is evaluated as follows, *-arr[1]-(-10)*⟹-0+10⟹10 (Arrays values are initialized with *0* during memory allocation. Minus * Minus = Plus). arr[1]+ = arr[1]+ = 10⟹arr[1] = arr[1]+10⟹arr[1] = 0+10⟹arr[1]=10.

17.
```
public class Test{
        public static void main(String[] args) {
            int A = 0x00FF;
            int B = 0x3333;
            System.out.println(A & B & A & B);
        }
}
```

Output:
51
Explanation:
0x00FF; 0000 0000 1111 1111
0x3333; 0011 0011 0011 0011
0x00FF; 0000 0000 1111 1111
0x3333; 0011 0011 0011 0011
============================
After AND operation:0000 0000 0011 0011
Enabled bits sum: 32 + 16 + 2 + 1 = 51

18.
```
public class Test        {
        public static void main(String Str[])    {
                int i=(2147483647 + 1);
                System.out.println(i);
        }
}
```
Output:
−2147483648

Explanation: *int* can occupy *32* bits (for 32 bits OS) in memory (from −2147483648 to +2147483647). In the above program, the sum of (2147483647 + 1) = 2147483648, which is higher than +2147483647. Thus, value will wrap around and reaches to -ve value.

19.
```
public class Test        {
        public static void main(String Str[])    {
                int i = ('A');
                System.out.println((char)i);
                int j = ( 'A' + 'B' ) − 'A';
                System.out.println( (char) j );
        }
}
```

Output:
A
B

Explanation: In Java, we can convert a character to int. Here, ASCII of 'A' is 65 and 'B' is 66 which is a *int*, while displaying them, it is type-casted back to char. Therefore above program is equivalent to below program.

```
class Test      {
        public static void main(String Str[])    {
                int i = (65);
```

```
            System.out.println((char)i);
            int j = ( 65 + 66) − 65;
            System.out.println( (char) j );
    }
}
Output:
A
B
```

```
20. public class Test{
        public static void main(String Str[])    {
            int i = ( 'A' + 'B' );
            String s=Integer.toString( 'A' + 'B' );
            System.out.println(i);
            System.out.println(s);
        }
}
Output:
131
131
```

Explanation: ASCII value of 'A' is 65 + ASCII value of 'B' is 66 = 131

```
21. public class Test{
        private static  boolean b = true;
        public static void main(String Str[])    {
                System.out.println(Str[0]+"Hello");
                if(b)    {
                        b=false;
                        main(new String[]{"Hi"});
                }
        }
}
```
Output of first run :
 <JAVA path>\bin>java Test
Exception in thread "main"
java.lang.ArrayIndexOutOfBoundsException: 0
at Test.main(Test.java:5)

Explanation: Array is empty and program is trying to access the elements in empty array. Hence leading to exception.

Output of Second run : <JAVA path>\bin>java Test ABC
ABCHello
HiHello

Explanation: The *main* method is used for recursion. If *main()* function is using for recursion, then we are shadowing *args* variable. Main function calls are placed on a stack, which has a finite place in memory; it can run out if it goes infinite. So, every time you call a function in Java, it goes onto the stack. We have to make sure that the recursion can end.

22.
```java
public class Test{
        private static void main(String main[]) {
                System.out.println("Hello");
        }
}
```

Output: Program compiles without error but fails while running and displays error, *"Main method is not public"*.

Explanation: Main method should have *public* visibility. Main method is called by JVM to run the method which is outside the scope of application hence the access specifier has to be *public* to allow call from anywhere outside the project. We also use *static* keyword, while JVM makes a call to the *main* method there is no instance existing for the class being called therefore it has to have static method to permit invocation from the class. Then come to return value from main, it returns void, because if it returns(as Java is platform independent language) a value then that may mean different to different platforms so unlike C it can not assume a behaviour of returning value to the OS.

23.
```java
public class Test{
        public static String main[]={"hi"};
        public static void main(String main[])  {
                System.out.println("main="+main[0]);
        }
}
```
Output of first run :
<JAVA path>\bin>java Test
Exception in thread "main"
java.lang.ArrayIndexOutOfBoundsException: 0
at Test.main(Test.java:5)

Output of Second run :
 <JAVA path>\bin>java Test hello
main=hello

Explanation:In the first run, array is empty and program is trying to access the elements in empty array, hence leading to exception. In the second run, sending command line argument while running a program.

```
24. public static void main(String args[])  {
            float[] arr = {(float)3.3, (float)4.4,(float)5.5,(float)6.6};
            float sum = 0;
            for (float f: arr) {
                sum += f;
            }
            System.out.println(" sum = "+sum);
    }
```

Output:
sum = 19.8

Explanation: This program is using enhanced *for* loop or for-each. The *for-each* loop is used to access each successive value in a collection of values. Above *for* loop is equivalent to *for (int i = 0; i < arr.length; i++)*. Enhanced *for* loop is a simpler way to do this same thing but little inflexible. Using enhanced loop, you do not require to know the index of the current element.

```
25. public class Test{
            public static void main(String args[]){
                    int i = 24;
                    int o = 030;
                    int h = 0x18;
                    System.out.println("i = "+i);
                    System.out.println("o = "+o);
                    System.out.println("h = "+h);
            }
    }
```
Output:
i = 24
o = 24
h = 24

Explanation: Decimal, octal and hexadecimal values are converted into *int* value respectively.

```
26. public class Test{
            public static void main(String args[])  {
                    String str1="";
                    String str2=null;
                    String str3=str2+str1;
                    String str4=str1+str2;
                    String str5=str1+"hi";
                    String str6="hi"+str2;
                    if(str1.equals(str2)){
                            System.out.println("str1=str2");
                    }
```

```
                       if(""".equals(str3)){
                               System.out.println("str1=str3");
                       }
                       System.out.println("str1="+str1);
                       System.out.println("str2="+str2);
                       System.out.println("str3="+str3);
                       System.out.println("str4="+str4);
                       System.out.println("str5="+str5);
                       System.out.println("str6="+str6);
               }
       }
```

Output:
```
str1=
str2=null
str3=null
str4=null
str5=hi
str6=hinull
```

Explanation: *null* is not a empty *String*. There are many ways to check whether a String is empty or not, few of them are,
1) *String.length()* can be used to check if the String length is 0.
2) *equals()* can be used to check a String is empty.
3) *isEmpty()* can be used to check a String is empty.
4) Using Apache commons *StringUtils* class, we can find if a String is empty.
5) We can check empty String using Spring framework's *StringUtils.hasLength()* method.

27.
```
public class Test{
}
```

Output:Compiles without error but fails while running and reports the following. Exception in thread *"main" java.lang. NoSuchMethodError:* main
Explanation: Java Virtual Machine uses *main* method as entry point when starts executing the code. Java code still compiles without *main* method, because this file's code may be missing a *main* method to become a a library instead of being executed.

28.
```
public class Test{
       public static void main(String args[])  {
               String a=null;
               if (a != null && a.length() > 1)
                       System.out.println("With &&");
               if (a!= null & a.length() > 1)
                       System.out.println("With &");
       }
}
```

Output: Compiles without error but fails while running. Error: Exception in thread *"main" java.lang.NullPointerException* at Test.main(Test.java:6)

Explanation: First *if* statement uses && and second *if* uses &, there is a difference between these two operators. You can see their differences in the below table,

&	&&
"bit-wise AND" operator	"Conditional logical AND" operator.
Ampercent (&) can be used as Bitwise operator.	AND operation is used for comparison operations.
Evaluates both arguments.	Evaluate the second argument, if the first argument is true.

29.
```java
public   class Test{
        public   static void main(String[] args) {
                int i = 1;
                int j = 2;
                if (i = j)
                        System.out.println("Not equal");
                else
                    System.out.println("Equal");
        }
}
```

Output: Test.java:5: error: incompatible types if (i = j) required: boolean found: int 1 error

Explanation: = is assignment operator, but *if* condition requires condition evaluation(boolean) operator(s), hence *if (i = j)* causes compilation to fail. You can avoid this error by using ==.

30.
```java
class TEST        {
        public static void main(String arg[])    {
                System.out.println(7*-+("Hello World first "
                .substring(6)+"program !").substring(6).length());
        }
}
```
Output: -105

Explanation: Resolve the display statement as follows, System.out.println(("Hello World first ".substring(6)+"program !").substring(6));

⇒"Hello World first ".substring(6)⇒ "World first "
⇒ "World first "+ "program !"
⇒ ("World first program !").substring(6) ⇒ "first program !"

The length of the string "first program !" is 15. Thus the expression after placing 15 from the length of the string becomes 7*-+15 == 7*(-15) == -105.

Note:7 * − + 15 will be translated into 7 * (−15) because (minus) * (plus) = minus.

31.
```java
import java.util.StringTokenizer;
class TEST        {
public static void main(String arg[])     {
        String str="15815.5825835.5";
        float sum=0;
        StringTokenizer tokens = new StringTokenizer(str);
        while(tokens.hasMoreElements()){
        sum=sum + Float.valueOf(
        (tokens.nextToken("8"))).floatValue();
        }
        System.out.println(sum);
        }
}
```
Output:91.0

Explanation: *StringTokenizer* basically used to break the string into tokens or words by using delimiters(in this example '8' is the delimiter). If delimiters are not specified, blanks are considered as the default delimiter. *StringTokenizer* constructor takes a string and breaks into tokens and returns a *StringTokenizer* object for that string. Each time, *nextToken()* method is called, it returns the next token in that string. The executing sequence of the code is as follows,
a) Tokenize the string based on delimiter.
b) Converting the string token into wrapper class *Float*.
c) Converting object numbers into primitive numbers (*float*).
d) Sum all the float values (sum = 15 + 15.5 + 25 + 35.5 = 91.0).

Note: *tokens. hasMoreTokens()* and *tokens.hasMoreElements()* performs same operation i.e.,returns *true* if there are more tokens available from tokenizing string argument. otherwise returns *false*.
Similarly, *tokens.nextToken()* and *tokens.nextElement()* performs same operation i.e, returns the next token from the tokenized string.

32.
```java
class TEST        {
        public static int val;
        static    {
                val=11;
                System.out.println("static_val="+val++);
        }
        public static void main(String arg[])     {
                System.out.println("main()_val="+val);
        }
}
```
Output:

```
static_val=11
main()_val=12
```

Explanation: Before executing *main*() function, it will execute the static block.
Note: A static variable belong to the class, shared by all class instances called class variables.

33.
```java
class TEST{
public static void main(String arg[])    {
        int a = 1;
        int b = 1;
        String aStr = new String("AB");
        String bStr = new String("CD");
        System.out.println(" a + b " + a+++b++);
        System.out.println(a+b + " a + b " );
        System.out.println("value: " + a + 0 );
        aStr += bStr;
        System.out.println("String: " + aStr + ++a + ++b );
        }
}
```
Output:
```
a + b 11
4 a + b
value: 20
String: ABCD33
```

Explanation: *a+++b++* is same as (a++)+(b++). Instruction *a+b* before ""(double quotes)adds the individual vales and displays the sum. But instruction a+b after ""(double quotes) displays the individual values.
Note: The + operator is used for both addition and concatenation operation.

34.
```java
class TEST        {
        public static void main(String arg[])    {
            int ch = 6;
            switch(ch)        {
                    case 1: System.out.println( "AB");
                    case 6: System.out.println(" CD");
                    default: System.out.println(" GH");
                                break;
                    case 4: System.out.println(" EF");
            }
        }
}
```
Output:
```
CD
GH
```

Explanation: Statements will be keep executing until it reaches *break* statement or until it encounters the end of the *switch* block.

Note: Default statement is executed if no case statements match and it can be written in anywhere within *switch* statement.

```
35. class  TEST        {
          public  static  void  main(String  arg[])     {
                  char  ch1='h';
                  char  ch2[]={ch1,'i'};
                  char  ch3[]=ch2;
                  String  str1="hi";
                  String  str2[]={"hello"};
                  String  str3[]={new  String(new  char[]{ch1})};
                  String  str4=new  String("hi");
                  System.out.println(ch1);
                  System.out.println(ch2);
                  System.out.println(ch3);
                  System.out.println(str1);
                  System.out.println(str2);
                  System.out.println(str3[0]);
                  System.out.println(str4);
          }
    }
    Output:
    h
    hi
    hi
    hi
    [java.lang.String;@16930e2
    h
    hi
```

Explanation: 5th time appearing *println* is prints the string which is name of the class of object instance along with the unsigned hexadecimal representation of hash code of the object.

Solution: To print the string appropriately use the index of it as follows,
System.out.println(str2[0]);
Note:String is a predefined class, not an array of characters.

e.g:
String s = "Hello"; // String
char[] a = 'H','e','l','l','o'; // array of characters

```
36. class  TEST        {
          public  static  void  main(String  arg[])     {
```

```
                              String  str  =  "Hello";
                              char[]  arr  =  {'H','e','l','l','o'};
                              String  newstr=str.replace('l',  'h');
                              char[]  newarr=arr;
                              arr[0]='h';
                              System.out.println(str);
                              System.out.println(newstr);
                              System.out.println(arr);
                              System.out.println(newarr);
                  }
      }
      Output:
      Hello
      Hehho
      hello
      hello
```

Explanation: Modifying the *String* object will not modify the original string, rather it returns a new modified string.

Note: *Strings* are read-only or immutable, i.e., once an object of the *String* class is created, the content of the string cannot be changed.

---

37.   class TEST
      {
      public static void main(String arg[])
      {
      System.out.println(5+6);
      System.out.println("5"+6);
      System.out.println(5+"6");
      System.out.println('5'+6);
      System.out.println(5+'6');
      System.out.println("1"+2+3);
      System.out.println(1+2+"3");
      }
      }
      Output:
      11
      56
      56
      59
      59
      123
      33

Explanation:
11→ 5+6=11.
56→ 6 is appending with string "5".

56→ string "6" is appending with 5.
59→ ASCII value of 5 is 53. Thus, 53+6=59.
59→ ASCII value of 6 is 54. Thus, 54+5=59.
123→ same like above.
33→ same like above.

38.
```
class TEST      {
       public static void main(String arg[])    {
              int i=10;
              String str1 = "x = " + i;
              String str2 = 2.7 + "";
              String str3 = 2.7;
           String str4 = "" + 2.7;
              String str5 = "" + i/2.7;
              System.out.println(str1+str2+str4+str5);
}
}
```

Output: TEST.java:6: error: incompatible types String str3 = 2.7; required: String found: double 1 error

Cause and Solution: *String str3 = 2.7;* is illegal as *str3* is a string. The *java.text.DecimalFormat* class provides many ways to format numbers into strings, including number of fraction digits, etc.

Output:
After removing the line no.6, you will get the below output.
x = 102.72.73.7037037037037033
Note: To round up the floating point numbers, *DecimalFormat* or the *Math.round* method can be used.

39.
```
class TEST      {
    public static void main(String arg[])    {
              int a = 10, b = 30;
              System.out.println(a + b);
              System.out.println(a + b + "1");
              System.out.println("2" + a + b);
              System.out.println("3" + a * b);
              System.out.println("3" + a - b);
              System.out.println("4" + a / b);
         }
}
```

Output:TEST.java:8: error: bad operand types for binary operator '-'
System.out.println("3" + a - b);
first type: String second type: int

Cause: Based on the operators priority, "3"+a is becomes a string. Therefore performing operation "String integer" is not allowed.

Solution: *System.out.println("3" +(a - b));*

Output:After correcting the above line, obtained below result.

```
40
401
21030
3300
3-20
40
```

Note: In the expression, there is *a* + operator, so the expression is evaluated left-to-right unless there were another operator with higher precedence.

```
40. 1.        class  TEST          {
    2.              public  static  void  main(String  arg[])      {
    3.                    short  s1=32767,s2=-32768;
    4.                    int  i=(byte)++s1;
    5.                    int  j=(byte)--s2;
    6.                    int  k=s1/(byte)s2;
    7.                    int  l=s2/(byte)s1;
    8.                    System.out.println("i="+ i+" j="+j);
    9.                    System.out.println("k="+ k+" l="+l);
    10.            }
    11.     }
```

Output: Exception in thread "main" java.lang.ArithmeticException: / by zero
at TEST.main(TEST.java:7)

Cause: Divide by zero error.

Solution:For run time exception handling, you can use *try-catch*. After correcting the above line, this program will run without any issue.

```
41. class  TEST  {
         public  static  void  main(String  arg[]){
              short  s1=32767,s2=-32768;
              int  i=(byte)++s1;
              int  j=(byte)--s2;
              int  k=s1/(byte)s2;
              int  l=s2/s1;
              try      {
                    l=s2/(byte)s1;
              }catch(ArithmeticException  ex)   {
              System.out.println("ERROR:DIVIDE  BY  ZERO");
```

```
                }
                System.out.println("i="+ i+" j="+j);
                System.out.println("k="+ k+" l="+l);
        }
}
```

Output:
ERROR: DIVIDE BY ZERO
i=0 j=-1
k=32768 l=0

Note:Mainly ArithmeticException are caused by math errors. The exception handling mechanism has fallowing tasks,

→Hit the exception.
→Throw the exception.
→Catch the exception.
→Handle the exception.

42.
```
class TEST        {
        public static void main(String arg[])    {
                String str1 = 2.7 + "";
                String str2 = "" + 2.7;
                String str3 = "2.7";
                String str4 = "3.7";

                if(str1==str2)
                        System.out.println("1");
                if(str1.equals(str2))
                        System.out.println("2");
                if(str1==str3)
                        System.out.println("3");
                if(str1.equals(str3))
                        System.out.println("4");
                if(str1==str4)
                        System.out.println("5");
                if(str1.equals(str4))
                        System.out.println("6");
        }
}
```
Output:
1
2
3
4

Explanation: Prefixing or suffixing of "" to a integer/float converts entire value into a string. We can use other techniques to convert a *int* to string, they are, *String.valueOf(number)* and *Integer.toString(number)*.

43.
```
class TEST
{
public static void main(String arg[])
{
byte b1=127,b2=-128;
b1++;b2--;
System.out.println("b1="+ b1+" b2="+b2);
}
}
```
Output: b1=-128 b2=127

Explanation: Typically a byte is an 8 bit integer data type. The range of the value of a byte is -128 to 127. If you add one to the maximum value of 127 turns to -128 and vice versa.

44.
```
class TEST
{
public static void main(String arg[])
{
int b1=127,b2=-128;
int i=(byte)++b1;
int j=(byte)--b2;
int k=b1;
int l=b2;
System.out.println("i="+ i+" j="+j);
System.out.println("k="+ k+" l="+l);
}
}
```
Output:
i=-128 j=127
k=128 l=-129

45.
```
class TestAA {
        int i;
        private int j;
                void set(int a, int b) {
                        i = a;
                        j = b;
                }
}
```

```
class TestBB extends TestAA    {
      int k=20;
}

class TEST    {
      public static void main(String args[])  {
            TestBB b=new TestBB ();
            b.set(10,20);
            System.out.println("The value of i"+b.i+"j="+b.j +"k="+b.k);
      }
}
```

Output: TEST.java:18: error: j has private access in TestAA
System.out.println("The value of i"+b.i+"j="+b.j +"k="+b.k);

Explanation: In class *TestAA*, *int j* is defined as *private*. Even though *TestBB* is a subclass of *TestAA*, it cannot inherit private members of super class *TestAA*. Class member that has been declared as *private* will remain *private* to its class. Hence it is not accessible by any code outside its class, which also includes subclasses.

46.
```
class Test {
        String str = "Test";
        Test(){}
        Test(String st){
                str=st;
        }

        void method() {
                InnerClass i = new InnerClass();
                i.innermethod();
                Test t=new Test("Hi");
                System.out.println(t.str);
                i.innermethod();
        }

        class InnerClass {
                public void innermethod() {
                        System.out.println(str);
                }
        }

        public static void main(String[] av) {
                Test p = new Test();
                p.method();
        }
}
```
Output:

Test
Hi
Test

Explanation: Objects that are instances of an inner class exist within an instance of the outer class. An inner class is associated with an instance of its surrounding class and has direct access to that object's methods and fields.

47.
```
public class TEST {
        public static void main(String args[])  {
        int a=1,b=2,c;
        System.out.println("Sum="+a+b+c);
        }
}
```

Output: TEST.java:4: error: variable c might not have been initialized
System.out.println("Sum="+a+b+c);

Explanation: Variable *c* has to initialize to some value before it's usage. We have declared *c*, but did not initialize them. Require to initialize c to a value. Initialization is required because it gets garbage value and further computation, behaviour can change it.

```
int c;        // This is a declaration
int c = 0;    // This is an initialization
```

48.
```
class Test {
        int x=10;
        Test()  {
                this(2);
        }
        Test(int x)     {
                this(x,x);
        }
        Test(int x,int y) {
                this();
                this.x=x+y;
        }

        public static void main(String args[])  {
                Test t=new Test();
                System.out.println("value ="+t.x);
                main(args);
        }
}
```
Output:
Test.java:9: error: recursive constructor Test(int x,int y) {...

Explanation: Recursive constructors are not allowed but recursive methods are allowed.

49.
```java
public class Test {
        int x = 10;
        Test(){
                this(x);
        }
        Test(int a){
                x = a;
        }
        public static void main(String args[]){
        Test t=new Test();
        System.out.println("value = "+t.x);
        }
}
```
Output:

Test.java:4: error: cannot reference x before supertype constructor has been called this(x);

Explanation: It is not possible to refer to not existing field before its declaration. Normally code inside constructors method will be computed as soon as object instance is created. Hence, declaration of *x* outside constructor is not visible inside constructor. Thus error.

50.
```java
public class Test {
        static int i = 10;       int j = 0;
        public  void Test (int k) {
                        System.out.println(i);
        }
        public static void main (String args []) {
              Test t = new Test(i);
              t.Test(i);
        }
}
```
Output:
Test.java:7: error: constructor Test in class Test cannot
 be applied to given types;   Test t = new Test(i);
                         ^
   required: no arguments
   found: int
   reason: actual and formal argument lists differ in length

Explanation: *public void Test (int k)* is not a constructor, as it is having return type. It is a normal method, hence *Test(int)* constructor is not defined in this class.

```
51. class Test {
        public void divOperation(int x, int y) {
            try {
                x=x / y;
            }catch (Exception e) {
                System.out.print("Caught exception, ");
            } finally {
                System.out.println("hit finally!");
            }
        }

        public static void main (String args []) {
            Test t=new Test();
            t.divOperation(1,0);
            t.divOperation(0,1);
        }
}
```

Output:
Caught exception, hit finally!
hit finally!

Explanation: The *finally* block always executes when the try block exits irrespective of exception throws. The *interrupt()* call will still result in the *finally* block being executed.

The *finally* cannot be called in these circumstances: if you use *System.exit()*, if the JVM crashes for some reason (e.g. infinite loop in the try block) or if a thread is stopped using the stop() method (or suspend() without resume()).

A *return* statement in the finally block will override any returns or exception throws in the try/catch blocks of the program.

```
52. class Vehicle {
        public void speed() {
            System.out.println("Vehicle-speed");
        }
}
class Car extends Vehicle {
        public void speed() {
            System.out.println("Car-speed");
        }
}

public class TEST {
        public static void main (String args []) {
            Vehicle v = new Vehicle();;
            Vehicle v1 = new Vehicle();;
            Car c = new Car();
            v.speed();
            c.speed();
```

```
                    v = c;
                    v.speed();
                    c=(Car)v1;
                    c.speed();
            }
    }
Output:
Vehicle-speed
Car-speed
Car-speed
Exception in thread "main" java.lang.ClassCastException:
 Vehicle cannot be cast to Car
         at TEST.main(TEST.java:21)
```

Explanation: *c = (Car)v1;* is not allowed, because the casting is allowed only in cases where a class extends a parent class and the child class is casted to its parent class, but *c = (Car)v1;* performing reverse.

53.
```
interface transport {
        public void speed() ;
}
class Vehicle implements transport{
        public void speed() {
                System.out.println("Vehicle-speed");
        }
}
class Car extends Vehicle   {
        public void speed() {
                System.out.println("Car-speed");
        }
}
public class TEST {
        public static void main (String args []) {
                Vehicle v=new Vehicle();
            transport v1=new Vehicle();
            transport c1=new Car();
                Car c= new Car();
                v.speed();
                c.speed();
                v = c;
                v.speed();
                c1=v1;
                c1.speed();
        }
}
Output:
Vehicle-speed
```

Car—speed
Car—speed
Vehicle —speed

Explanation: Abstract method *speed()* in *transport* interface is implemented in *Vehicle* class, again *speed()* method is overridden in *Car* class.

```
54. class Employee{
            String name;
            int sal;
            Employee(String name , int sal){
                    this.name=name;
                    this.sal=sal;
            }
            public void method(){
                    System.out.println(this.name);
                    System.out.println(this.sal);
            }
    }
    public  class TEST {
            public static void main (String args []) {
                    Employee emp=null;
                    try{
                            emp = new Employee("ABC", 1200);
                            emp.method();
                    } finally {
                            System.gc();
                            emp.method();
                    }
            }
     }
     Output:
     ABC
     1200
     ABC
     1200
```

Explanation: The *java.lang.System.gc()* runs the garbage collector, it is a request to a Java Virtual Machine to regain the unused object's memory but this is not guarantee that when *gc* thread runs. Calling *System.gc()/Runtime.gc()* is not fully reliable, sometime garbage-collection thread might defer to a thread of higher priority.

```
55. public class Test {
            public void method1(int x) {
                    loop: for (int i = 1; i < 3; i++){
```

```java
                    for (int j = 1; j < 3; j++) {
                            System.out.println("Method1:"+i * j);
                            if (x == 1) {
                            break loop;
                            }
                    }
            }
    }
    public void method2(int x) {
            for (int i = 1; i < 3; i++){
            for (int j = 1; j < 3; j++) {
                    System.out.println("Method2:"+i * j);
                    if (x== 1) {
                    break ;
                    }
            }
            }
    }
    public static void main (String args []) {
            Test t=new Test();
            t.method1(1);
            t.method2(1);
    }
}
Output:
Method1:1
Method2:1
Method2:2
```

Explanation: The unlabeled *break* statement terminates the innermost *for* loop, *switch, while loop, or do-while* loop statement. But a labeled *break* terminates moves the control to statement following label.

```java
56. public  class Test {
    public void method1(int x) {
            switch (x) {
            default:
                    System.out.print(1+",");
            case 1:
                    System.out.print(2+",");
            case 2:
            case 3:
                    System.out.print(3+",");
            case 4:
                    System.out.print(4);
            }
    }
    public void method2(int x) {
```

```
                          switch (x) {
                          case 1:
                                  System.out.print(2+",");
                          case 2:
                          case 3:
                                  System.out.print(3+",");
                          case 4:
                                  System.out.print(4+",");
                          default:
                                  System.out.print(1);
                          }
                  }
          public static void main (String args []) {
                  Test t = new Test();
                  t.method1(5);
                  System.out.println("");
                  t.method1(1);
                  System.out.println("");
                  t.method2(5);
                  System.out.println("");
                  t.method2(1);
          }
  }
Output:
1,2,3,4
2,3,4
1
2,3,4,1
```

Explanation: The default section handles all values that are not explicitly handled by the *switch* condition. In the above program *break* statement is missing, hence control flow is not terminated until end of *switch* block.

```
57. class A {
          public A (String str) {
                  System.out.println(str);
          }
  }
  public class Test extends A {
          public static void main(String args []) {
                  Test t=new Test();
          }
  }
Output:
Test.java:6: error: constructor A in class A cannot
be applied to given types;
class Test extends A {
```

```
required: String
found: no arguments
reason: actual and formal argument lists differ in length
```

Explanation: Default constructor *A()* is missing in *class A*. If you created a constructor for a class, then there won't be any default constructor created. Hence, if a subclass extends that class and tries to call the no-argument constructor of its parent class then we notice a compile-time error.

58.
```java
public class  Test {
        public static void Test() {
                print(true);
        }
        public static void print(boolean f) {
                f = !f;
                if (f = true) {
                        System.out.println ("TRUE");
                }
                else {
                        System.out.println ("FALSE");
                }
        }
        public static void main(String args []) {
                Test();
        }
}
```
Output:
TRUE

Explanation: *f = !f;* ⇒ *f=false* but *if* statement has *f = true* (assignment operator (=), not logical operator (==)). Thus, *if* condition is *true*, hence prints "TRUE".

What happens if we write like: *boolean result = false && (false)?false:true* ? It returns true !. The above code is equivalent to *boolean result = (false && false)?false:true;* and ternary operator (?:) has lower precedence than &&. Since *false && false* is *false*, which reduces to *boolean result = false ? false : true;* which ideally produce *true*.

59.
```java
public class  Test {
        public  Test() {
                method();
        }
        public  void method1() {
                System.out.println ("A");
        }
        public static void method() {
```

```
                    System.out.println("B");
                    method1();
            }
            public static void main(String args []) {
                    Test t=new Test();
            }
    }
```
Output:

Test.java:10: error: non-static method method1() cannot be referenced from a static context method1();

Explanation: In Java, static methods or class methods cannot call non-static methods. An instance of the class is required to call non-static methods. Also, static methods are not associated with an instance.

```
60. public class  Test {
            public  void method() {
                    StringBuffer sb = new StringBuffer("ABC");
                    String s = new String("ABC");
                    if(sb.equals(s)){
                            System.out.println("A");
                    }
                    if(sb.toString().equals(s)){
                            System.out.println("B");
                    }
                    if(sb.equals(new StringBuffer(s))){
                            System.out.println("C");
                    }
                    if(sb.toString().
                    equals(new StringBuffer(s).toString())){
                            System.out.println("D");
                    }
            }
            public static void main(String args []) {
                    Test t=new Test();
                    t.method();
            }
    }
```
Output:
B
D

Explanation: *sb.equals(s)*⟹ *sb* and *s* are different objects, hence comparison is invalid.
sb.toString().equals(s)⟹ The value of *sb* is converted into *String* and then comparing with *String s* makes proper comparison.
sb.equals(new StringBuffer(s))⟹ This statement is comparing same object types but different object references. Here it is not comparing *String* values. *sb.toString(). equals(new StringBuffer(s).toString())*⟹ converts into String and compares both values. This makes exact value comparison.

```
61. public class  Test {
         Test(){
                  System.out.println("default constructor");
         }
         Test(int i){
                  System.out.println("constructor,i="+i);
         }
         static {
                  System.out.println("static block");
                  Test();
         }

         public static void Test() {
                           System.out.println("static method");
         }

         public static void main(String args []) {
                  Test t = new Test();
                  t.Test();
                  Test t1 = new Test(10);
                  t1.Test();
         }
}
```
Output:
static block
static method
default constructor
static method
constructor,i=10
static method

Explanation: Static block will be executed as soon as first class is loaded into a Java Virtual Machine. When the class is first accessed, the *static* initializer for a class gets run, then either to create an instance or to access a *static* method or field.

```
62. public class  Test {
         public static void main(String args []) {
                  System.out.println("A");
                  /*System.out.println("B");
                    System.out.println("C");
                  /*System.out.println("D");*/
                  System.out.println("E");
         }
}
```

Output:
A
E

Explanation: Any code within the comments will be ignored by the compiler. Java supports single line(implementation comments), multi-line(implementation comments), and Java-doc(documentation) comments. Single line(end-of-line) comments are used for one lines explanation. Multi-line comments(slash-star comments) are called block comments which is used when more than one line of comments are written. Lastly, Javadoc comments are inserted to describe classes, interfaces, fields, methods, or constructors.

63.
```java
import java.util.Vector;
public class  Test {
        public static void main(String args []) {
                String str1 = "A";
                String str2 = "B";
                Vector vct = new Vector();
                vct.add(str1);
                vct.add(str2);
                String str3 = vct.elementAt(0) + vct.elementAt(1);
                System.out.println(str3);
        }
}
```
Output:
Test.java:9: error: bad operand types for binary operator '+'
String str3 = vct.elementAt(0) + vct.elementAt(1);
   first type: Object
   second type: Object
Note: Test.java uses unchecked or unsafe operations.
Note: Recompile with −Xlint:unchecked for details.

Explanation: Type casting is required during object assignment. e.g., *vct.elementAt(0) + vct.elementAt(1);* should be written as *(String)vct.elementAt(0) + vct.elementAt(1);*

64.
```java
public class  Test {
        public static void main(String args []) {
                String str = new String("ABC");
                String s[]= {new String("AB"),new String("CD")};
                int i=str.length();
                int j=s.length;
                System.out.println("i="+i);
                System.out.println("j="+j);
        }
}
```
Output:

i=3
j=2

Explanation: The *length* keyword is used to find out the array length and *length()* method is used find out the *String* length. See differences in the below table. An array holds a fixed number of values of a single type. Array's length never changes after an array is created. The length of array is presented as a final instance variable length. An array can be created using an expression and initializer. The size is specified when array is created.

length	length()
The *length* field is used to find out the array length/size.	The *length()* method is used to find out the *String* length.
Example: String s[]={new String("AB"), new String("CD")}; int j=s.length; System.out.println("j="+j);	Example: String str=new String("AB"); int i=str.length(); System.out.println("i="+i);

65.
```
class A {
        public   abstract void method() {
                System.out.println("Hi");
        }
}
class  Test extends A {
        public static void main(String args []) {
                Test t=new Test();
                t.method();
        }
}
```
Output:
Test.java:1: error: A is not abstract and does not override abstract method method() in A
class A {
Test.java:2: error: abstract methods cannot have a body
        public   abstract void method(){

Explanation: If any method in the class is declared as *abstract* then the class has to be declared *abstract* and the method has to be implemented in the following subclass(s). Hence, declare above class as *abstract* class. Abstract methods do not specify the body. The methods of abstract class must always be redefined in a subclass called overriding and defining the methods in subclass is mandatory. Abstract class can have non-abstract methods. Further, non-abstract methods need not be overridden in the subclass.

66.
```
abstract class A{
        abstract void method();
}
class   Test extends A {
        void method1(){
                System.out.println("Hi");
        }
        public static void main(String args []) {
                Test t=new Test();
                t.method();
        }
}
```
Output:
```
Test.java:4: error: Test is not abstract and does not override abstract
 method method() in A
 class   Test extends A {
```

Explanation: Abstract methods of base class have to be implemented in the derived subclass(s). Hence *method*() has to implement in class *Test*.

67.
```
abstract class A{
        void method(){
                System.out.println("Class A");
        }
}
  class   Test extends A {
        void method(){
                System.out.println("Hi");
        }
        public static void main(String args []) {
                Test t = new Test();
                t.method();
                A t1 = new A();
        }
}
```
Output:
```
Test.java:13: error: A is abstract; cannot be instantiated
                A t1 = new A();
```

Explanation: When a class is declared as *abstract* we can't instantiate it. Remove *A t1 = new A();* to avoid compiler error. An abstract class can only be inherited from. Either we need to remove the *abstract* keyword from the class definition or remove *A t1 = new A();*.

68.
```
abstract class A {
        void method(){
                System.out.println("Class A");
        }
}
public class  Test extends A {
        void method(){
                System.out.println("Hi");
        }
        public static void main(String args []) {
                Test t=new Test();
                t.method();
                ((A)t).method();
        }
}
```
Output:
Hi
Hi

Explanation: Object *t* is the instance of *Test*, which is derived from base class *A* and *method()* is implemented in subclass. Hence it will execute the program.

69.
```
abstract class A {
        void method(){
                System.out.println("Class A");
        }
}
public class  Test extends A {
        public static void main(String args []) {
                Test t=new Test();
                t.method();
                ((A)t).method();
        }
}
```
Output:
Class A
Class A

Explanation: Default behaviour is considered when there is no implementation in derived/subclasses.

70.
```
interface  interf{
        public void method();
}
abstract class A implements interf{
```

```
        public void method(){
                System.out.println("Class A");
        }
}
public class  Test extends A {
        private void method(){
                System.out.println("Hi");
        }
        public static void main(String args []) {
                Test t=new Test();
                t.method();
        }
}
```

Output:
Test.java:10: error: method() in Test cannot implement method()
in interf private void method(){
attempting to assign weaker access privileges; was public

Explanation: If *abstract* class has public method and its visibility cannot be reduced in the inherited method of a class. Here *private void method()* should be converted into *public void method()*.

71.
```
interface  interf{
        public abstract void method();
}
abstract class A {
        public abstract void method();
}

public class  Test extends A implements interf{
        public void method(){
                System.out.println("Hi");
        }
        public static void main(String args []) {
                Test t=new Test();
                ((interf)t).method();
                ((((t)))).method();
        }
}
```
Output:
Hi
Hi

Explanation: We require to satisfy both conditions at once, that is, implementation of fulfilling the *abstract* class requirements and the interface requirements.

```
72. interface  interf{
          public abstract int method();
    }
    abstract class A {
          public abstract void method();
    }

    public class  Test extends A implements interf{
          public void method(){
                System.out.println("Hi");
          }
          public int method(){
                System.out.println("Hello");
                return 0;
          }
          public static void main(String args []) {
                Test t=new Test();
                ((interf)t).method();
                t.method();
          }
    }
```

Output:
Test.java:12: error: method method() is already defined in
class Test public int method(){
Test.java:8: error: Test is not abstract and does not
override abstract method method() in interf
class Test extends A implements interf{
Test.java:9: error: method() in Test cannot implement
method() in interf public void method(){
return type void is not compatible with int

Explanation: Same method name is trying to override with different return values hence error, we can avoid this error if we return same type from *method()*. A method in abstract class has to provide its implementation in the first concrete class where it extends. With this task, we need to provide implementation of interface for the method. If both the methods differ only in return type, the concrete class will try to overload the methods which differ only in return type but unfortunately we can not have overloaded methods which differ only in return type, therefore we notice such errors.

```
73. interface  interf{
          public abstract void method(){
                System.out.println("Hi");
          }
    }
    public class  Test implements interf{
          public void method(){
                System.out.println("Hello");
          }
```

```
        public static void main(String args []) {
                Test t=new Test();
                t.method();
                ((interf)t).method();
        }
}
```
Output:
Hello
Hello

Explanation: Even though interface method has a body, it does not prevent to compile and run the program.

74.
```
interface  interf{
        public abstract void method(){
        System.out.println("Hi");
        }
}
public class  Test implements interf{
        public static void main(String args []) {
                Test t=new Test();
                ((interf)t).method();
        }
}
```
Output:
```
Test.java:2: error: interface methods cannot have body
public abstract void method(){
Test.java:6: error: Test is not abstract and does not override
abstract method method() in interf
class  Test implements interf{
```

Explanation: Interface will never provide default behaviour, however, *abstract* class will provide default behaviour. Hence all methods in the interface class are *abstract* by default and it has to be implemented in implementer classes.

75.
```
public class  Test {
        static{
                try{

                }catch(Exception exe){
                        try{

                        }catch(Exception e){

                        }finally{
```

```
                                    }
                            }
                            finally {
                                    System.out.println ("Hi");
                            }
                    }
                    public static void main(String args []) {
                    }
            }
```

Output:
Hi

Explanation: *static* block will be executed first by default without explicit calling and *finally* block is executed irrespective of control flow in the *try-catch* block. The *finally* block always executes soon after control exits from *try* block. This ensures that the *finally* block is executed even if an unexpected exception occurs while running the program. It allows the developer to avoid having clean-up code accidentally bypassed by either *return*, *continue* or *break*.

76.
```
public class  Test {
            static private final    int k = 10;
            static final  private   int l = 10;
            final static private    int m = 10;
            final  private static   int n = 10;
            private static  final   int o = 10;
            private final  static   int p = 10;

            public  void  method( final int k){
                    System.out.println (k);
                    System.out.println (l);
                    System.out.println (m);
                    System.out.println (n);
                    System.out.println (o);
                    System.out.println (p);
            }
            public static void main(String args []) {
                    Test t = new Test ();
                    t.method (20);
            }
}
```
Output:
20
10
10
10
10
10

Explanation: Basically *private*, *static* and *final* are modifier keywords and they can be placed in any order for variable declarations.

77.
```java
class A{
        public void methodA(){
                System.out.println("A");
        }
}

public class  Test extends A {
        public  void  methodA( ){
                System.out.println("Test");
                super.methodA();
        }

        public  void  methodA(int i ){
                System.out.println("i="+i);
        }
        public  void  methodA( char c){
                System.out.println("c="+c);
        }

        public static void main(String args []) {
                Test t = new Test();
                t.methodA();
                t.methodA(10);
                t.methodA('A');
                ((A)t).methodA();
                A a = new A();
                a.methodA();
        }
}
```
Output:
Test
A
i=10
c=A
Test
A
A

Explanation: Class *Test* is overriding a method called *methodA( ){}* and has overloading methods like, *methodA(int i){}* and *methodA(char i){}*. Base class or super class method can be called by using *super* keyword.

78. ```java
class A{
        public final void methodA(){
                System.out.println("A");
        }
}
public class Test extends A {
        public final void methodA( ){
                System.out.println("Test");
                super.methodA();
        }
        public static void main(String args []) {
                Test t = new Test();
                t.methodA();
        }
}
```
Output:
Test.java:7: error: methodA() in Test cannot override
methodA() in A public  final void  methodA( ){
overridden method is final

Explanation: Final method cannot be overridden but overloading a *final* method is allowed.

---

79. ```java
final class A{
        public  void methodA(){
                System.out.println("A");
        }
}
public class  Test extends A {
        public  final void  methodA( final int  i ){
                System.out.println("i="+i++);
                }
        public static void main(String args []) {
                Test t = new Test();
                t.methodA(10);
        }
}
```
Output:
Test.java:6: error: cannot inherit from final A
 class Test extends A {

Explanation: Final variable acts like a constant and value cannot be changed from its initiated value. Similarly *final* class cannot get subclassed.

80. ```java
final abstract class A{
        public abstract void methodA();
```
```

```
}
public class  Test extends A {
        public  final void  methodA(  int  i ){
                System.out.println("i="+i++);
        }
        public  static void main(String  args  []) {
                Test  t = new Test();
                t.methodA(10);
        }
}
```

Output:
Test.java:1: error: illegal combination of modifiers:
abstract and final final abstract class A{
Test.java:4: error: cannot inherit from final A
 class Test extends A {
Test.java:4: error: Test is not abstract and does not override
abstract method methodA() in A
 class Test extends A {

Explanation: A class can be either *final* or *abstract*, but not both. Important points to remember about *final* keyword in Java,

(a) Final keyword is applicable to local variable, member variable, method or class in Java.

(b) Final member variable should be initialized while declaration or inside constructor, if not done so, we notice a compilation error.

(c) Local *final* variable should be initialized during declaration.

(d) Reassign value to *final* variable is not possible.

(e) Inside anonymous class, only *final* variable is accessible.

(f) Final class cannot be inheritable.

(g) Final method cannot be overridden.

(h) Final and *abstract* are two opposite keywords and a final class cannot be abstract.

(i) Final and *finally* are different keywords, *finally* keyword which is used on Exception handling.

(j) Final and *finalize()* are different keywords, *finalize()* called before an object is garbage collected by JVM.

(k) All variable declared within a interface are implicitly *final*.

(l) Final methods have *static* binding while compile time.

(m) Making a class, method or variable *final* helps to improve performance because JVM gets an chance to make assumption and optimization.

(n) Usually *final* variables are treated as constants and written in all Caps e.g. *private final int SIZE=100;*

(o) If a collection reference variable is *final*, only reference cannot be modified but you can add, remove or change object inside collection.

81.
```
class A{
        void A(){
                System.out.println("A");
        }
         A(){
                System.out.println("B");
        }
}
public class  Test extends A {
        Test(){
                super();
                super.A();
        }
        public static void main(String args []) {
                Test t = new Test();
                t.A();
        }
}
```
Output:
B
A
A

Explanation: *super();* calls constructor of base class and *super.A();* calls the method of base class. The *super()* calls the base class's constructor with no arguments but it can be used also with arguments. Example: super(arg1), this will call the constructor that accepts one parameter of the type of *arg1*. Usually, *super* refers to immediate base class's instance variables and methods.

82.
```
class A{
        private static int i=10;
        public   static int j=20;
}
public class  Test {
        public static void main(String args []) {
                System.out.println(A.i);
                System.out.println(A.j);
        }
}
```
Output:
Test.java:7: error: i has private access in A
                System.out.println(A.i);

Explanation: Public variable/method is accessible to members of any class. Private variable/method are not visible from outside the class.

```
83. abstract class A{
            private void method1() {
                    System.out.println("A");
            }
            public abstract void method2() ;
    }
    public class  Test extends A {
            public void method2(){
                    System.out.println("B");
            }
            public static void main(String args []) {
                    Test t=new Test();
                    t.method1();
                    t.method2();
            }
    }
    Output:
     Test.java:13: error: cannot find symbol
                    t.method1();
       symbol:    method method1()
       location: variable t of type Test
```

Explanation: Visibility modifier in *abstract* class can be *public* or *protected*. Generally *private* methods cannot inherit properties or they are not polymorphic, hence it does not make sense to have a *private* method *abstract*. Abstract means, you have to override and implement it in a subclass, but as you cannot override *private* methods, you cannot make them *abstract* either. We can make it protected instead of *private*. Typically, *private* means *private* to a class you have defined the method in; even subclasses don not access *private* methods. If a method declaration that contains the keyword *abstract* also contains any one of the keywords *private, static, native, strictfp, final* or *synchronized* will result in a compile-time error.

```
84. interface inter {
            public void method() ;
    }
    public class Test implements inter  {
            public static void main(String args []) {
                    Test t=new Test();
                    t.method();
            }
    }
    Output:
    Test.java:4: error: Test is not abstract and does not
    override abstract method method() in inter  class Test
    implements inter  {
    Test.java:7: error: cannot find symbol  t.method();
       symbol:    method method()
       location: variable t of type Test
```

Explanation: A class which implements an interface must implement all of the methods of a interface. When a class is defined to implement an interface, the class must provide definitions of all the methods defined in the interface. Otherwise, you will get compiler time error.

A class have to implement all the methods of an interface, if not the class is declared as abstract. When you declare the class as an abstract, then it forces you to subclass the class and implements the missing methods prior to creating any objects.

In a case, where class do not require implementing all methods in the interface is when any class in its inheritance tree has previously given concrete (non-abstract) method implementations then the subclass is under no requirement to re-implement those methods. The derived class may not implement the interface whatsoever and just method signature is matched.

In the below code, a concrete class *Derived* that declares that it implements an interface *Interf*, but does not implement *Method()* method of the interface. The code is permissible because its parent class *Base* implements a method called *Method()* with the same name as the method in the interface *Interf*. Example:

```java
interface Interf {
  void Method() throws NullPointerException;
}
class Base {
//NOTE : Base class doesn't implements Interf interface
  public void Method() {
    System.out.println("Base Method()");
  }
}

class Derived extends Base implements Interf {
}

class Test {
  public static void main(String args[]) {
    Derived s = new Derived();
    s.Method();
  }
}
Output:
Base Method()
```

85.
```java
interface inter {
        public final void method() ;
}
public class Test implements inter {
        public void method(){
                System.out.println("A");
        }
        public static void main(String args []) {
                Test t = new Test();
```

```
                t.method();
        }
}
Output:
Test.java:2: error: modifier final not allowed here
public  final  void method()  ;
```

Explanation: Final methods cannot be overridden. Implicitly Java override interface methods.

86.
```
interface  inter {
        private  void method()  ;
}
public class  Test implements inter  {
        public void method(){
                System.out.println("A");
        }
        public static void main(String args []) {
                Test t=new Test();
                t.method();
        }
}
Output:
Main.java:2: error: modifier private not allowed here
private  void method()  ;
```

Explanation: Private cannot be used in interface. Java can compile and runs a program despite methods of interface have *public* or *abstract* visibility.

87.
```
interface  inter {
        public  void method()  ;
}
class  A implements inter {
}
public class  Test extends A  {
        public void method(){
                System.out.println("A");
        }
        public static void main(String args []) {
                Test t=new Test();
                t.method();
        }
}
Output:
A
```

88.
```
interface   inter {
        public void method();
        final private int i = 10;
}
public class Test implements inter {
        public final void method(){
                System.out.println("A");
        }
        public static void main(String args []) {
                Test t=new Test();
                t.method();
        }
}
```
Output:
```
Test.java:3: error: modifier private not allowed here
        final private int i = 10;
```

Explanation: Only *public*, *static* and *final* are keywords permitted for variables/fields in the interface.

89.
```
class A {
        A(){
                System.out.println("A");
        }
}
public class  Test extends A {
        public Test(){
                System.out.println("B");
        }
        public static void main(String args []) {
                Test t=new Test();
        }
}
```
Output:
A
B

Explanation: No need to make a explicit call to default constructor of base class, because it will be supplied automatically.

```
public Test(){
        super();
        System.out.println("B");
}
```

is same as

```
    public Test(){
            System.out.println("B");
    }
```

90.
```
class A {
        A(){
                System.out.println("A");
        }
}
public class  Test extends A {
        public Test(){
                System.out.println("B");
                super();
        }
        public static void main(String args []) {
                Test t=new Test();
        }
}
```
Output:
```
Test.java:9: error: call to super must be first statement
 in constructor super();
```

Explanation: Calling the constructor for the base class must be the first statement in the body of a constructor.

91.
```
class A {
        A(){
                System.out.println("A");
        }
        A(char c ){
                System.out.println(c);
        }
}

public class Test extends A {
        public Test(){
                super();
        }
        public Test(char i){
                super(i);
        }
        public  Test(int i,int j){
                this ();
        }
```

```
    public   Test(int i,int j,int k){
              this('c');
    }
    public static void main(String args []) {
              Test t=new Test();
    }
}
```
Output:
A

92.
```
class A {
        A(){
                System.out.println("A");
        }
}
public class  Test extends A {
        public   Test(){
                super();
                super();
        }
        public static void main(String args []) {
                Test t=new Test();
        }
}
```
Output:
Test.java:9: error: call to super must be first statement
 in constructor super();

Explanation: Java enforces to call *super* (explicit or not) should be the first statement in the constructor. Helps to prevent the derived class part of the object being initialized before to the base-class part of the object being initialized.

93.
```
public class  Test extends Object {
        public static void main(String args []) {
                Test t=new Test();
                Object o=new Object();
                if(t.getClass().equals(o.getClass())){
                        System.out.println("Hi");
                }else{
                        System.out.println("Hello");
                }
        }
}
```
Output:
Hello

Explanation: All classes in Java directly or indirectly inherit from *Object* class. *Object* class is an exception to this rule and has no base-class. So, all classes implicitly extend the *Object* if no other base-class is given. On other hand, interfaces do not extend *Object* since it cannot have invokable methods, nor can objects be instantiated from them. *Object* implements no interfaces.

94.
```java
import java.util.*;
public class Test{
public static void main(String[] args) {
    TreeMap <Integer, String>mp = new TreeMap<Integer, String >();
        TreeMap mp1 = new TreeMap();
        mp.put(5, "Z");
        mp.put(7, "A");
        mp.put(2, "B");
        mp1.put("Z", "12");
        mp1.put("A", "2");
        mp1.put("D", "32");
        mp1.put("E", "22");
        System.out.println("Keys of mp: " + mp.keySet());
        System.out.println("Values of mp: " + mp.values());
        System.out.println("Keys of mp1: " + mp1.keySet());
        System.out.println("Values of mp1: " + mp1.values());
        }
}
```
Output:
Keys of mp: [2, 5, 7]
Values of mp: [B, Z, A]
Keys of mp1: [A, D, E, Z]
Values of mp1: [2, 32, 22, 12]

Explanation: Content of tree map will be sorted either by their natural order or comparator using keys.

95.
```java
import java.util.*;
public class Test{
        public static void main(String[] args) {
            TreeMap mp = new TreeMap();
            mp.put(3, "Z");
            mp.put(1, 3);
            mp.put(2, 'c');
            System.out.println("Keys of mp: " + mp.keySet());
            System.out.println("Values of mp: " + mp.values());
        }
}
```
Output:
Keys of mp: [1, 2, 3]
Values of mp: [3, c, Z]

96.
```java
import java.util.*;
class Test{
        public static void main(String[] args) {
            TreeMap mp = new TreeMap();
            mp.put(3, "Z");
            mp.put('c', 3);
            mp.put("A", 'c');
            System.out.println("Keys of mp: " + mp.keySet());
            System.out.println("Values of mp: " + mp.values());
        }
}
```
Output:
Exception in thread "main" java.lang.ClassCastException:
 java.lang.Integer
cannot be cast to java.lang.Character   at Test.main
(Test.java:6)

Explanation: Data type for keys should be same across the given tree map.

97.
```java
import java.util.*;
public class Test{
        public static void main(String[] args) {
            TreeMap mp = new TreeMap();
            mp.put(String.valueOf(3), "Z");
            mp.put(Integer.valueOf('c').toString(), 3);
            mp.put("A", 'c');
            System.out.println("Keys of mp: " + mp.keySet());
            System.out.println("Values of mp: " + mp.values());
        }
}
```
Output:
Keys of mp: [3, 99, A]
Values of mp: [Z, 3, c]

98.
```java
import java.text.DecimalFormat;
import java.text.NumberFormat;
import java.util.*;
public class Test{
        public static void main(String[] args) {
            TreeMap mp = new TreeMap();
```

```
            int  c=10;
            NumberFormat format = new DecimalFormat("1000");
            mp.put(format.format(Integer.parseInt( "11")),
            String.format("%06d", 12));
            mp.put(format.format(Integer.parseInt( "21")), 'B');
            mp.put(format.format(Integer.parseInt( "13")), c);
            System.out.println("Keys of mp: " + mp.keySet());
            System.out.println("Values of mp: " + mp.values());
        }
}
```

Output:
Keys of mp: [1011, 1013, 1021]
Values of mp: [000012, 10, B]

Explanation: Numeric and String formatting is used.

99.
```
import java.util.*;
class Test{
        public static void main(String[] args) {
                TreeMap mp = new TreeMap();
                mp.put("GH", new Float(123.45));
                mp.put("AC", new Float(456.78));
                mp.put("FD", new Float(789.12));
                Set set = mp.entrySet();
                Iterator i = set.iterator();
                while(i.hasNext()) {
                        Map.Entry me = (Map.Entry)i.next();
                        System.out.print(me.getKey() + ": ");
                        System.out.println(me.getValue());
                        mp.remove("AC");
                }
        }
}
```

Output:
AC: 456.78
Exception in thread "main" java.util.ConcurrentModificationException
        at Test.main(Test.java:12)

Explanation: Interpreter has detected concurrent modification of an object where as such modification is not permissible. It is not a synchronization issue, this will happen if the underlying collection that is being iterated over is modified by anything other than the Iterator itself. The resolved program is given below,

```
import java.util.*;
class Test{
        public static void main(String[] args) {
                TreeMap mp = new TreeMap();
                mp.put("GH", new Float(123.45));
```

```
            mp.put("AC", new Float(456.78));
            mp.put("FD", new Float(789.12));
            Set set = mp.entrySet();
            Iterator i = set.iterator();

            while(i.hasNext()) {
                    Map.Entry me = (Map.Entry)i.next();
                    System.out.print(me.getKey() + ": ");
                    System.out.println(me.getValue());
                    i.remove();
            }
        }
}
```

```
100. import java.util.*;
     class Test{
             public static void main(String args[]) {
             HashMap mp = new HashMap();
             mp.put("A", new Integer(123));
             mp.put("A", new Integer(123));
             mp.put("Z", new Integer(456));
             mp.put("Z", new Integer(456));
             mp.put("B", new Integer(789));
             mp.put("B", new Integer(789));
             System.out.println("Keys of mp: " + mp.keySet());
             System.out.println("Values of mp: " + mp.values());
             }
     }
     Output:
     Keys of mp: [A, B, Z]
     Values of mp: [123, 789, 456]
```

Explanation: Duplicates are eliminated.

```
101. import java.util.*;
     class Test {
             public static void main(String args[]) {
                     HashMap mp = new HashMap();
                     mp.put("A", new Integer(123));
                     mp.put("", new Integer(124));
                     mp.put(null, new Integer(125));
                     Set set = mp.entrySet();
                     Iterator i = set.iterator();
```

```
            while(i.hasNext()) {
                    Map.Entry me = (Map.Entry)i.next();
                    System.out.print(me.getKey() + ": ");
                    System.out.println(me.getValue());
            }
        }
}
```
Output:
```
null: 125
: 124
A: 123
```

Explanation: Null and "" are different in the context of Java. Though it is not relent here to discuss about "" and null, it makes sense to understand what they are. Say *String str1 = "";* means that the empty String is assigned to *str1*. Then *str1.length()* is the same as *"".length()*, which will give 0 as expected. Lets take *String str2 = null;* which means that null or "no value at all" is assigned to *str2*. So, *str2.length()* is the same as *null.length()* witch will result in a NullPointerException since you can not access methods on null variables. *String str1;* is same as *String str1 = null;*

102.
```
class Test {
        public   String method(int i){
                return (""+i);
        }
        public static void main(String args[]) {
                System.out.println(method(100));
        }
}
```
Output:
```
Test.java:6: error: non-static method method(int) cannot
be referenced from a static context
System.out.println(method(100));
```

Explanation: A *static* method can only call other *static* method.

103.
```
import java.util.*;
class Test {
public static void main(String args[]) {
        HashMap mp = new HashMap();
        mp.put("A", new Integer(1));
        mp.put("", new Integer(2));
        mp.put(null, new Integer(3));
        mp.put("",null);
        mp.put(null, "");
        mp.put(null, null);
```

```
                System . out . println (mp. get ("")  );
                System . out . print (mp. get ( null )  );
        }
}
Output :
null
null
```

Explanation: Maps can accept a *null* key and *null* values. Further, latest values overlaps previous value if duplicate existed.

104.
```
import java . util .*;
class Test extends HashMap {
        public static void main(String args []) {
                HashMap mp = new HashMap ();
                mp. put (' ', new Integer (1));
                System . out . println (mp. get ('\b')  );
        }
}
Output :
null
```

Explanation: Key is not found in a HashMap hence null. ASCII of backspace is 8, please see below snippet's output if you replace in the program,

```
mp. put ('\b', new Integer (1));
System . out . println (mp. get ('\b')  );
Output :1
```

```
mp. put (" ", new Integer (1));
mp. put (( char )8, new Integer (2));
System . out . println (mp. get ('\b')  );
Output :2
```

105.
```
import java . util .*;
class Test {
        public static void main(String args []) {
                Hashtable ht = new Hashtable ();
                Enumeration en ;
                String str ;
                ht. put ("4", new Double (12.12));
                ht. put ("3", new Double (34.56));
                ht. put ("6", new Double (78.89));
                en = ht. keys ();
```

```
                    while(en.hasMoreElements()) {
                            str = (String) en.nextElement();
                            ht.remove(str);
                            System.out.println(str + ": " +
                            ht.get(str));
                    }
            }
}
```
Output:
6: null
4: null
3: null

Explanation: In *Hashtable* you can change the iteration and exception will not be thrown. Like the *HashMap* classes, *Hashtable* does not directly support iterators. Hence, the program uses an enumeration to display the contents of *ht*. However, you can obtain set-views of the hash table, which permits the use of iterators.

106.
```
import java.util.*;
class Test {
        public static void main(String args[]) {
                Hashtable <String, Double>ht =
                new Hashtable<String, Double>();
                Enumeration <String>en;
                String str;
                ht.put("4", new Float(12.12));
                ht.put("3", new Double(34.56));
                ht.put("6", new Double(78.89));
                en = ht.keys();
                while(en.hasMoreElements()) {
                        str = (String) en.nextElement();
                        System.out.println(str + ": " +
                        ht.get(str));
                }
        }
}
```
Output:
```
Test.java:8: error: no suitable method found for put(String,Float)
ht.put("4", new Float(12.12));
method Hashtable.put(String,Double) is not applicable
(actual argument Float cannot be converted to Double by
 method invocation conversion)
```

Explanation: Here, the problem is that we are trying to place a *Float* literal in a map having *String* as key, *Float* as value.

```
107. import java.util.*;
     class Test{
             public static void main(String args[]) {
                     Hashtable <String, Double>ht =
                     new Hashtable<String, Double>();
                     ht.put("4", new Double(12.12));
                     ht.put("3", new Double(34.56));
                     ht.put("6", new Double(78.89));
                     Hashtable <String, Double>ht1 =
                     new Hashtable<String, Double>(2);
                     ht1.put("7", new Double(12.12));
                     ht1.put("9", new Double(34.56));
                     ht1.put("8", new Double(78.89));
                     Hashtable <String, Double>ht2 =
                     new Hashtable<String, Double>(2,(float).1);
                     ht2.put("2", new Double(12.12));
                     ht2.put("1", new Double(34.56));
                     ht2.put("3", new Double(78.89));
                     HashMap mp = new HashMap();
                     mp.put("A", new Integer(1));
                     mp.put("B", new Integer(2));
                     mp.put("C", new Integer(3));
                     Hashtable <String, Double>ht3 =
                     new Hashtable<String, Double>(mp);

                     System.out.println("Keys of mp:"+ht.keySet());
                     System.out.println("Values of mp:"+ht.values());
                     System.out.println("Keys of mp:"+ht1.keySet());
                     System.out.println("Values of mp:"+ht1.values());
                     System.out.println("Keys of mp:"+ht2.keySet());
                     System.out.println("Values of mp:"+ht2.values());
                     System.out.println("Keys of mp:"+ht3.keySet());
                     System.out.println("Values of mp:"+ht3.values());
             }
     }
Output:
Keys of mp: [6, 4, 3]
Values of mp: [78.89, 12.12, 34.56]
Keys of mp: [9, 8, 7]
Values of mp: [34.56, 78.89, 12.12]
Keys of mp: [3, 2, 1]
Values of mp: [78.89, 12.12, 34.56]
Keys of mp: [A, C, B]
Values of mp: [1, 3, 2]
```

```
108. import java.util.*;
```

```
class Test {
        public static void main(String args[]) {
                Hashtable <String, Double>ht =
                new Hashtable<String, Double>(2,(float)0.0);
                ht.put("7", new Double(12.12));
                ht.put("9", new Double(34.56));
                ht.put("8", new Double(78.89));
                System.out.println("Keys of mp:"+ht.keySet());
                System.out.println("Values of mp:"+ht.values());
        }
}
```

Output:
Exception in thread "main" java.lang.IllegalArgumentException:
Illegal Load: 0.0
at Test.main(Test.java:4)

Explanation: Creating a hash table that has an initial size specified by *size* and a fill ratio specified by *fillRatio*.

109.
```
import java.util.EnumMap;
enum enm{ONE,TWO ,THREE}
public class TEST {
        void test() {
                emp.put(enm.THREE, 1000);
                emp.put(enm.ONE, 2000);
                System.out.println(emp.get(enm.ONE)*emp.
                get(enm.THREE));
        }
    private EnumMap<enm,Integer> emp =
    new EnumMap<enm,Integer >(enm.class);
    public static void main(String[] args) {
        Test eg = new Test();
        eg.test();
    }
}
```
Output:
2000000

Explanation: A simpler computation, 2000*1000=2000000.

110.
```
import java.util.*;
class Test {
        public static void main(String args[]) {
                HashSet <String>hs = new HashSet<String >();
                HashSet <String>hs1 = new HashSet<String >();
```

```
                hs.add("4");
                hs.add("1");
                hs.add("3");
                hs.add("2");
                hs1=hs;
                System.out.println(hs.equals(hs.remove("10")));
                System.out.println("hs:"+hs);
                System.out.println(hs1.equals(hs));
                System.out.println("hs1:"+hs1);
                hs.remove("1");
                System.out.println("hs:"+hs);
                System.out.println("hs1:"+hs1);
        }
}
```
Output:
```
false
hs:[3, 2, 1, 4]
true
hs1:[3, 2, 1, 4]
hs:[3, 2, 4]
hs1:[3, 2, 4]
```

Explanation: A *HashSet* is an unsorted and unordered set. It uses the hashcode of the object being inserted.

111.
```
import java.util.*;
class Test {
        public static void main(String args[]) {
                HashSet hs = new HashSet();
                hs.add("4");
                hs.add(hs);
                hs.add("2");
                hs.add("2");
                System.out.println("hs:"+hs);
        }
}
```
Output:
```
hs:[2, (this Collection), 4]
```

Explanation: Duplicates are eliminated in *HashSet*.

112.
```
import java.util.HashSet;
import java.util.Iterator;
public class Test {
        public static void main( String[] args )          {
```

```
                        HashSet  hs  =  new  HashSet ();
                                hs.add (" 1 ");
                                hs.add (" 2 ");
                                hs.add (" 3 ");
                                Iterator  iter  =  hs.iterator ();

                                while (iter.hasNext ())  {
                                        System.out.println (iter.next ());
                                iter.remove ();
                                }
                }
        }
        Output:
        3
        2
        1
```

```
113. import  java.util.HashSet;
     import  java.util.Iterator;
     public    class Test        {
                public static void main ( String [] args )              {
                        HashSet  <String >hs  =  new  HashSet<String >();
                hs.add (" 1 ");
                        hs.add (" 2 ");
                hs.add (" 3 ");

                        Iterator  <String >iter  =  hs.iterator ();
                        {
                            System.out.println (iter.next ());
                            iter.remove ();
                        }
                }
        }
        Output:
        3
```

```
114. import  java.util.Iterator;
     import  java.util.TreeSet;
     public  class  Test{
                public static void main ( String [] args )              {
                        TreeSet<String >hs  =  new  TreeSet<String >();
                hs.add (" 1 ");
                        hs.add (" 2 ");
```

```
                        hs.add("3");
                Iterator <String>iter = hs.iterator();
                        while(iter.hasNext()) {
                        System.out.println(iter.next());
                        iter.remove();
                }
        }
}
Output:
1
2
3
```

115.
```
import java.util.Iterator;
import java.util.TreeSet;
public class Test        {
        public static void main( String[] args )              {
                TreeSet<TreeSet>hs = new TreeSet<TreeSet >();
        hs.add(hs);
                Iterator iter = hs.iterator();
        while(iter.hasNext()) {
                        System.out.println(iter.next());
                iter.remove();
                }
        }
}
Output:
[(this Collection)]
```

116.
```
import java.util.Iterator;
import java.util.TreeSet;
public class Test {
        public static void main( String[] args ) {
                TreeSet <TreeSet<TreeSet<TreeSet>>>hs = new TreeSet();
                TreeSet hs1 = new TreeSet();
                hs1.add("Hi");
        hs.add(hs1);
        Iterator iter = hs.iterator();
        while(iter.hasNext()) {
                        System.out.println(iter.next());
                iter.remove();
                }
        }
```

```
        }
Output:
[Hi]
```

117.
```
import java.util.Iterator;
import java.util.LinkedHashMap;
import java.util.Set;
public class Test {
        public static void main(String[] args) {
                LinkedHashMap hm = new LinkedHashMap();
                hm.put("","A");
                hm.put("","B");
                hm.put("","C");
                Set st = hm.keySet();
                Iterator itr = st.iterator();
                while(itr.hasNext()){
                        System.out.println(itr.next());
                }
        }
}
```
Output: No output generated from this program.

118.
```
import java.util.*;
class Test {
        public static void main(String args[]) {
            LinkedHashSet hs = new LinkedHashSet();
            hs.add("3");
            hs.add("2");
            hs.add("1");
            hs.add("5");
            System.out.println(hs.contains('1'));
        }
}
```
Output: false

Explanation: In *hs.contains('1')*, ASCII of 1 is searched in a set, but did not find it. The correct way of searching is *hs.contains("1");*

```
119. import java.util.EnumSet;
     public class Test {
             enum Letter  { A,B,C,D };
             public static void main(String[] args) {
         EnumSet<Letter> i = EnumSet.of(Letter.A, Letter.B);
         EnumSet<Letter> j = EnumSet.range(Letter.C, Letter.D);
         EnumSet<Letter> k = EnumSet.complementOf(j);
         EnumSet<Letter> l = EnumSet.allOf(Letter.class);
                 if(i.contains(Letter.A))
                     System.out.println("A is there !");
                 if(!i.contains(Letter.C))
                     System.out.println("C is not there !");
                 for(Letter s : j)
                     System.out.println(s);
         }
         public static boolean canGoToMoes(EnumSet<Letter> m) {
         return !m.contains( EnumSet.range(Letter.A, Letter.B) );
         }
     }
     Output:
     A is there !
     C is not there !
     C
     D
```

```
120. public class Test extends Thread implements Runnable{
             public static int count=0;
             public Test(String str) {
                     super(str);
             }

             public void run()    {
                     for (int i = 0; i < 10; i++) {
                     count=count+i;
                     }
                     System.out.println("val="+count);
             }

             public static void main(String[] args){
                     new Test("ABC").start();
         new Test("DEF").start();
             }
     }

     Output:
     val=45
```

val=90

Explanation: Sum of numbers from 0 to 9.

121.
```
public class Test extends Thread{
        public static int count=0;
        public Test(String str) {
                super(str);
        }
        public static void run()
        {
        System.out.println("val="+count);
        }
        public static void main(String[] args){
                new Test("ABC").start();
        }
}
```
Output:
```
Test.java:6: error: run() in Test cannot implement run() in Runnable
public static void run()
overriding method is static
```

Explanation: Static keyword cannot be used for *run* method, if you remove static keyword, then it works fine.

122.
```
interface interf1{
        abstract public void method();
}
interface interf2 extends interf1{
        abstract public void method();
}
class A implements interf1{
        public void method(){
                System.out.println("1");
        }
}
class Test extends A implements interf1, interf2{
        public void method(){
                System.out.println("2");
        }
        public static void main(String[] args){
                Test t=new Test();
                t.method();
```

```
                    A a=new A();
                    a.method();
                    ((interf1)t).method();
                    ((interf2)t).method();
                    ((interf1)a).method();
                    ((interf2)a).method();
            }
    }
```

Output:

2

1

2

2

1

Exception in thread "main" java.lang.ClassCastException:
A cannot be cast to interf2 at Test.main(Test.java:24)

Explanation: Class *A* is not implementing *interf2*. Hence above exception is thrown.

```
123. interface interf1{
            abstract public void method();
    }
    interface interf2 extends interf1{
            abstract public void method();
    }
    class A {
            A(int i){
                    this.method();
            }
            A(){
                    A a=new A(1);
                    a.method();
            }
            public void method(){
                    System.out.print("1,");
            }
    }
    public class Test extends A implements interf1 , interf2{
            Test(){
                    super();
            }
            public void method(){
                    System.out.print("2,");
            }
            public static void main(String[] args){
                    Test t=new Test();
                    t.method();
```

```
                        A a=new A();
                        a.method();
                        ((interf1)t).method();
                        ((interf2)t).method();
                }
        }
}
Output:
1,1,2,1,1,1,2,2,
```

```
124. public class Test implements Runnable  {
            private String name;
            private long time;

            public Test(String name, long time)    {
                    this.name = name;
                    this.time = time;
            }

            public static void main (String[] args) {
                    Thread t = new Thread(new Test("ABC",1));
                    t.setDaemon(true);
                    t.start();
                    Thread t1 = new Thread(new Test("DEF",1));
                    t1.setDaemon(true);
                    t1.start();

                    try    {
                            System.in.read();
                    }

            catch (Exception e)     {
                            System.out.println("Exception "+e);
                    }
            }

            public void run(){
                    int i=0;
                    do {
                            System.out.println(name);
                            try {
                                    Thread.sleep(time);
                            }
                            catch (Exception e)     {
                            System.out.println("Exception "+e);
                            }
                    }while(i--!=0);
```

```
                }
        }
        Output:
        ABC
        DEF
```

125.
```
import java.io.*;
import java.util.*;
public class Test
{
  public static void main (String[] args)
   throws java.io.IOException
  {
   String str;
   int i = 1;
   BufferedReader br = new BufferedReader
   (new FileReader ("D:/test/abcTest/src/Test.java"));
   while(true){
           str= br.readLine();
           if(str==null)
                   break;
            System.out.println ("Line$\sharp1$"+i+++":"+str);
   }
  }
}
Output:
Line$\sharp1$:import java.io.*;
Line$\sharp1$2:import java.util.*;
Line$\sharp1$3:public class Test
Line$\sharp1$4:{
Line$\sharp1$5: public static void main (String[] args)
                               throws java.io.IOException
Line$\sharp1$6: {
Line$\sharp1$7:  String str;
Line$\sharp1$8:  int i = 1;
Line$\sharp1$9:  BufferedReader br = new BufferedReader
(new FileReader ("D:/test/abcTest/src/Test.java"));
Line$\sharp1$10:  while(true){
Line$\sharp1$11:          str= br.readLine();
Line$\sharp1$12:          if(str==null)
Line$\sharp1$13:                  break;
Line$\sharp1$14:System.out.println ("Line$\sharp1$"+i+++":"+str);
Line$\sharp1$15:  }
Line$\sharp1$16:  }
Line$\sharp1$17:}
```

126.
```java
import java.io.*;
public class Test           {
    public static void main (String[] args) throws
            java.io.IOException      {
        String str;
        boolean flag = true;
        BufferedReader br = new BufferedReader
                (new InputStreamReader (System.in));
        FileWriter fw = new FileWriter
                ("D:/test/abcTest/src/Text.txt");
        BufferedWriter bw = new BufferedWriter (fw);
        PrintWriter pw = new PrintWriter (bw);
        while ( flag ) {
                System.out.println ("Enter the input String.");
            str = br.readLine ();
                if (str.length() == 0)
                flag = false;
                else
                        pw.println (str);
        }
        pw.close ();
        System.out.println ("Your Data is here:");
        int i = 1;
        BufferedReader br1 = new BufferedReader (
        new FileReader ("D:/test/abcTest/src/Text.txt"));
        while (true){
                str= br1.readLine ();
                if (str==null)
                        break;
                System.out.println ("Line$\sharp1$"+i+++":"+
                        str.toUpperCase());
        }
    }
}
```
Output:
Enter the input String.
aaaaa
Enter the input String.
bbbbb
Enter the input String.
CCCCC
Enter the input String.
<ENTER nothing>
Your Data is here:
Line$\sharp1$1:AAAAA
Line$\sharp1$2:BBBBB
Line$\sharp1$3:CCCCC

127.
```
public class Test {
    public static void main (String[] args) throws Exception {
        System.out.println(0/0);
        throw new Exception("Test Exception");
    }
}
```
Output:

Exception in thread "main" *java.lang.ArithmeticException*: / by zero at Test.main(Test.java:3)

Explanation: Control flow has not reached throw exception code. It has failed before reaching that line.

128.
```
public class Test {
    public static void main(String args[]) {
        Runtime rt = Runtime.getRuntime();
        int numOfProcessors = rt.availableProcessors();
        System.out.println(numOfProcessors + "
        processor(s) are available to JVM");
    }
}
```
Output:

Two processors are available for JVM

Explanation: *availableProcessors()* method of runtime returns the number of processors currently available for the JVM.

129.
```
public class Test {
    public static void main(String args[]) {
        Runtime rt = Runtime.getRuntime();
        System.out.println("Maximum memory
        available to JVM is:"+rt.maxMemory() + " bytes");
    }
}
```
Output:

Maximum memory available for JVM is *259522560* bytes

Explanation: *maxMemory()* method of Runtime calculates the maximum amount of memory available to JVM.

```
130. public class Test {
     public static void main(String args[])  {
             Runtime.getRuntime().gc();
             System.out.println("Running Garbage Collector...");
             }
     }
```
Output:

Running Garbage Collector...

Explanation: *gc()* method of Runtime class suggest the JVM to run garbage collection.

```
131. import java.util.Properties;
     public class Test {
             public static void main(String[] args) {
                     String OS = System.getProperty("os.name");
                     String JavaVersion = System.getProperty(
                     "java.specification.version");
                     Properties properties = System.getProperties();
             if(OS != null)   {
             if(OS.toLowerCase().indexOf("windows") != -1)
                     System.out.println("Your OS is Windows...");
             else
                     System.out.print("Your OS is not windows...");
             }
             System.out.println("Java Version : " + JavaVersion);
             System.out.println("Properties of System:");
             properties.list(System.out);
             }
     }
```
Output:
Your OS is Windows...
Java Version : 1.7
Properties of System:
--listing properties
--<prints all properties of current system>

```
132. public  class Test {
     public static void main(String[] args) {
             StringBuffer strbuf = new StringBuffer(
             new String(new String("ABC ")));
             strbuf.append("DEF");
             System.out.println("Append Operation:"+strbuf);
             int len = strbuf.length();
```

```
                System.out.println("Length Operation:"+len);
                String str = strbuf.substring(5);
                System.out.println("Substring Operation: " + str);
                String str1 = strbuf.substring(0,5);
                System.out.println("Substring Operation: " + str1);
                strbuf.replace(0,5,"AB");
                System.out.println("Replace Operation: " + strbuf);
                strbuf.insert(3,"ABCD ");
                System.out.println("Insert Operation:"+strbuf);
                strbuf.deleteCharAt(1);
                System.out.println("Delete Operation:"+strbuf);
                strbuf.reverse();
                System.out.println("Reversed Operation: " + strbuf);
        }
}
```
Output:
Append Operation:ABC DEF
Length Operation:7
Substring Operation: EF
Substring Operation: ABC D
Replace Operation: ABEF
Insert Operation:ABEABCD F
Delete Operation:AEABCD F
Reversed Operation: F DCBAEA

133.
```
import java.util.LinkedList;
public class Test {
        public static void main(String[] args) {
        LinkedList<String> ll = new LinkedList<String>();
        LinkedList<LinkedList<String>> lll =
                new LinkedList<LinkedList<String>>();
                ll.add("B");
                ll.add("C");
                ll.add("D");
                ll.addFirst("A");
                ll.addLast("E");
                lll.add(ll);
                System.out.println(lll.contains("F") &&
                 lll.remove().equals("A"));
                System.out.println("Linked List:" + lll);
        }
}
```
Output:
false
Linked List:[[A, B, C, D, E]]

134.
```
import java.util.StringTokenizer;
public class Test {
    public static void main(String[] args) {
        StringTokenizer st1=new StringTokenizer("AB|CD", "|");
        while(st1.hasMoreTokens()){
            System.out.println(st1.nextToken());
        }
        StringTokenizer st2 = new StringTokenizer("EF|GH");
        while(st2.hasMoreTokens()){
            System.out.println(st2.nextToken("F"));
        }
    }
}
```
Output:
AB
CD
E
|GH

135.
```
import java.util.StringTokenizer;
public class Test {
    public static void main(String[] args) {
        StringTokenizer st = new StringTokenizer(
        "Hello world !", " ");
        String strReversedLine="";
        while(st.hasMoreTokens()){
            strReversedLine = (st.nextToken().
            toLowerCase() + " " +
             strReversedLine.toUpperCase()).
             replace("HELLO", "Hi");
        }
        System.out.println(strReversedLine);
    }
}
```
Output:! WORLD HI

136.
```
public class Test {
    public static void main(String[] args) {
        Double i = Double.valueOf(Float.valueOf(
```

```
        Integer . valueOf
        (Short . valueOf ("1"). toString ()). toString ()).
        toString ());
        System . out . println ( i );
    }
}
Output: 1.0
```

137.
```
public class Test {
    public static void main(String [] args) {
        Double i = Double . valueOf ( Float . valueOf (
        Integer . valueOf
        (Short . valueOf ("1.0"). toString ()). toString ()).
        toString ());
        System . out . println ( i );
    }
}
```
Output:
```
Exception in thread "main" java . lang . NumberFormatException:
For input string: "1.0"
        at java . lang . NumberFormatException . forInputString
        (NumberFormatException . java :65)
        at java . lang . Integer . parseInt ( Integer . java :492)
        at java . lang . Short . parseShort ( Short . java :117)
        at java . lang . Short . valueOf ( Short . java :173)
        at java . lang . Short . valueOf ( Short . java :199)
        at Test . main ( Test . java :3)
```

Explanation: It is an unchecked exception which can happen when you are attempting to convert a *String* to a numeric value, like an *Float* or an *Integer*, but the String is not well formatted for the conversion. If you are trying to parse an integer but the string is something like "1.0", then conversion will fail with a *NumberFormatException*.

138.
```
import java . util . ArrayList ;
import java . util . Collections ;
import java . util . Comparator ;

class intComparator implements Comparator{
    public int compare(Object obj1 , Object obj2 ){
        int obj1Val = (( Integer )obj1 ). intValue ();
        int obj2Val = (( Integer )obj2 ). intValue ();
        if ( obj1Val > obj2Val )
        return 1;
        else if ( obj1Val < obj2Val )
```

```
                    return -1;
                    else
                    return 0;
                    }
          }
      class Test {
        public static void main(String[] args) {
                ArrayList <Integer>arrList = new ArrayList<Integer >();
                arrList.add(2);
                arrList.add(4);
                arrList.add(1);
                arrList.add(3);
                Collections.sort(arrList ,new intComparator ());
                System.out.println(arrList);
        }
}
Output:
[1, 2, 3, 4]
```

139.
```
import java.util.ArrayList;
import java.util.Collections;
import java.util.Comparator;
public class Test {
    public static void main(String[] args) {
            ArrayList <Integer>arrList = new ArrayList<Integer >();
            arrList.add(2);
            arrList.add(4);
            arrList.add(1);
            arrList.add(3);
            Comparator <Integer>comparator = Collections.reverseOrder ();
            Collections.sort(arrList ,comparator );
            System.out.println(arrList );
    }
}
Output: [4, 3, 2, 1]
```

140.
```
import java.util.ArrayList;
import java.util.Vector;
public class Test {
    public static void main(String[] args) {
            Vector <String>vect = new Vector<String >();
            vect.add("A");
            vect.add("C");
```

```
            vect.add("E");
            ArrayList <String>arrList = new ArrayList<String >();
            arrList.add("B");
            arrList.add("D");
            vect.addAll(1,arrList);
            vect.remove("A");
            for(int i=0; i<vect.size(); i++)
            System.out.print(vect.get(i)+" ");
    }
}
Output: B D C E
```

```
141. import java.util.*;
     import java.lang.*;
     import java.io.*;
     class Program {
             private int id;
             public Program (int id) {
                     this.id = id;
             }
             public int hashCode() {
                     return id;
             }
             public boolean equals (Object obj) {
                     return (this == obj) ? true : super.equals(obj);
             }
             public boolean equals (int obj) {
                     return (this.id == obj) ? true : super.equals(obj);
             }
     }

     public class Test {
       public static void main(String[] args) {
             Program p1 = new Program(100);
             Program p2 = new Program(100);
             Program p3 = new Program(200);
             System.out.print(p1.equals(p1) + " ");
             System.out.print(p1.equals(p2) + " ");
             System.out.print(p1.equals(100) );
       }
     }
Output:
true false true
```

Explanation: Object reference comparison rather than it's value, hence above output.

```
142. import java.util.*;
     import java.lang.*;
     import java.io.*;
     class B {
       void method() {
             System.out.println("B");
       }
     }
     class A extends B{
       void method() {
             System.out.println("A");
       }
     }
     public class Test        {
       public static void main (String[] args) throws
        java.lang.Exception   {
             A A = new A();
             ((B)A).method();
             A C = new A();
             ((B)C).method();
             B B = new B();
             ((B)A).method();
             B D = new B();
             ((B)D).method();
       }
     }
     Output:
     A
     A
     A
     B
```

```
143. import java.util.*;
     public class Test {
       public static void main(String[] args) {
             List<Integer> L = new <Integer>ArrayList();
             L.add(11);
             L.add(22);
             L.add(33);
             L.add(44);
             L.add(Integer.valueOf(L.get(-0).toString()));
             System.out.println(L);
       }
     }
     Output: [11, 22, 33, 44, 11]
```

144.
```java
import java.util.Scanner;
class Test {
    public static void main (String[] args) {
        Scanner S1 = new Scanner(System.in);
        String ch = S1.next();
        System.out.println("1st str=" + ch);
        int ch1 = S1.nextInt();
        System.out.println("2nd int=" + ch1);
        float ch2 = S1.nextFloat();
        System.out.println("3rd float=" + ch2);
    }
}
```
Input: 10 20 30.33
Output:
1st str=10
2nd int=20
3rd float=30.33

145.
```java
import java.util.*;
import java.lang.*;
import java.io.*;
class Clz {
        int a = 10;
        String method1() {
                return "clz1";
        }
        protected static String method2 () {
                return "clz2";
        }
}

class Test extends Clz {
        int a = 20;
        String method1() {
                return "test1";
        }
        public static String method2() {
                return "test2";
        }
        void method() {
                Clz m = new Test();
                System.out.print(m.method1()+ " "+
                m.method2() +" "+ m.a);
```

```
            }
            public static void main (String [] args) {
                    new Test ().method ();
            }
    }
    Output: test1  clz2  10
```

146.
```
    public class Test{
            public static void main(String srgs []){
                    static int i=10;
                    System.out.println(i);
            }
    }
    Output:
    Test.java:3: error: illegal start of expression
    static int i=10;
```

Explanation: Static variables are defined at class level. It cannot be declared inside a method.

147.
```
    public class Test {
        public static void main(String [] args) {
            int a=1000,b=2000;
            a^=b^=a^=b;
            System.out.println (a+":"+b);
            a=1000;b=2000;
            b=a^=b=b^a^b;
            System.out.println (a+":"+b);
        }
    }
    Output:
    0:1000
    0:0
```

148.
```
    class T
    {
        final public int method(int a, int b) { return 0; }
    }
    class T1 extends T
    {
        public int method(int a, int b) {return 1; }
```

```
    }
public class Test
{
    public static void main(String args[])
    {
        T1 b = new T1();
        System.out.println(b.method(10, 20));
    }
}
```
Output:
```
Main.java:7: error: method(int,int) in T1 cannot
 override method(int,int) in T
    public int method(int a, int b) {return 1; }
  overridden method is final
```

Explanation: Cannot override *final* method.

149.
```
public class Test {
        public static void main(String[] args) {
                int a=10,b='a';
                System.out.println(true ?a:b);
                System.out.println(false?a:b);
        }
}
```
Output:
```
10
97
```

150.
```
class Test {
    public static void main(String [] args){
        Test t = new Test();
        t.m();
    }

    void m(){
        int [] a1 = {10,20,30};
        int [] a2 = method(a1);
        System.out.println(a1[0] + a1[1] + a1[2]);
        System.out.println(a2[0] + a2[1] + a2[2]);
    }

    int [] method(int [] a){
        a[1] = 40;
        return a;
```

```
        }
}
Output:
80
80
```

151.
```
class Test {
    public static void main(String [] args){
        Test t = new Test();
        t.m();
    }

    void m(){
        String str1 = "5678";
        String str2 = method(str1);
        System.out.println(str1 + str2);
    }

    String method(String s1){
        s1 = s1 + "1234";
        System.out.println(s1);
        return "1234";
    }
}
Output:
56781234
56781234
```

152.
```
public class Test {
    public static void main(String[] args) {
        int a=123456;
        short b=0;
        System.out.println(b+=a);
    }
}
Output:-7616
```

Explanation: Size of short is between -32768 to 32767(system dependent), after rotation of 123456 for short size, then we will reach -7616.

```
153. class Test {
        public static void main(String [] args) {
            int i = 0x80000000;
            System.out.println(i);
            i = i >>> 31;
            System.out.println(i);
            i = i << 31;
            System.out.println(i);
        }
    }
```
Output:
```
-2147483648
1
-2147483648
```

Explanation: Size of *int* is 32 bits and it's size ranges from 2,147,483,648 to 2,147,483,647(system dependent). In the above program, 0x80000000 is equivalent to 2,147,483,648 which is higher than 2,147,483,647, so rotates back 2,147,483,648.
Example:

```
int a = 0x80; // produce 128
byte b = (byte) a; // produce -127
```

or

```
char c = (char) 0xffff;
c++;
System.out.println((int) c); // 0
```

Hence *i* has a value 1000 0000 0000 0000 0000 0000 0000 0000(2,147,483,648) >>> is used to Logical shift. Zeros are shifted in to replace the discarded bits. Operator moves the bits towards right with sign bit. After moving 31 bits, we get 1 as value of *i*.

```
154. public class Test {
            public static void main(String[] args) {
                System.out.println(0*20000000 +0xabcafebe);
                System.out.println(0*20000000L+0xabcafebeL);
            }
    }
```
Output:
```
-1412759874
2882207422
```

Explanation: Observe below table(32 bit OS), in first println, 0*20000000 +0xabcafebe = -1412759874, see how computation done, basically it perform integer computation rather than Long computation, so 0*20000000 = 0 and 0xabcafebe => 2882207422 which is higher than 2,147,483,647, hence after rotating values, 2,882,207,422 - 2,147,483,647 - 2,147,483,647 => -1412759874.
In second *println*, it computes Long values, so 0xabcafebe => 2882207422.

Name	Width	Range
long	64	-9,223,372,036,854,775,808 to 9,223,372,036,854,775,807
int	32	-2,147,483,648 to 2,147,483,647
short	16	- 32,768 to 32,767
byte	8	- 128 to 127

155.
```java
class Test {
        public static void main(String [] args) {
                int i = 22;
                float f = (float)22.1;
                boolean b = (i == f);
                System.out.println(b);
                int c=20;
                String str = (c < 15) ? "Hi" : (c < 22)? "hello" : "1234";
                System.out.println(str);
        }
}
```
Output:
```
false
hello
```

Explanation: The answer is straight, 22 is not equal to 22.1, so result is false. Next evaluation is ternary operator where c is >15 and < 22, so result is "hello".

156.
```java
class Test {
        public static void main(String [] args) {
        int i= 10;
        int j= 10;
        for (int a = 0; a < 10; a++) {
            if (( ++i > 2 ) && (++j > 2)) {
                i++;
            }
        }
        System.out.println(i + " " + j);
        int k= 20;
        int l= 20;
        for (int a = 0; a < 10; a++) {
            if (( ++k > 2 ) || (++l > 2)) {
```

```
                    k++;
            }
        }
        System.out.println(k + " " + 1);
        int m = 21 & 22;
        int n = m ^ 2;
        System.out.println( n | 10 );
    }
}
```
Output:
30 20
40 20
30

```
157. class Test {
        public static void main(String [] args) {
        boolean a = true;
        boolean b = false;
        boolean c = true;
        if ( a & b | b & c | b )
            System.out.print("A");
        if ( a & b | b & c | b | a )
            System.out.println("B");
            }
    }
```
Output:B

Explanation:

a & b | b & c | b => false | false | false =>false.
a & b | b & c | b | a => false | false | false | true => true

---

```
158. class Test {
        static int stat;
        public static void main(String [] args) {
        Test t = new Test();
        t.method();
        System.out.println(stat);
    }
        void method() {
        int a = 20;
        m(a);
        System.out.print(a + " ");
```

```
        }

                void m( int  a)  {
                        a  =  a*2;
                        stat  =  a;
                }
}
Output :  20    40
```

```
159. class A {
        byte  i;
    }

    class Test {
        public  static  void  main(String  []  args)  {
                        Test  t  =  new  Test();
                        t.method();
        }

        void  method()  {
                        A  a  =  new  A();
                        System.out.println(a.i);
                        A  b  =  m(a);
                        System.out.println(a.i  +  ″  ″  +  b.i);
        }
        A m(A  a)  {
                        a.i  =  10;
                        return  a;
        }
    }
Output:
0
10  10
```

```
160. class Test {
            boolean  []  b  =  new  boolean[10];
        int  i  =  0;

        void  method(boolean  []  a,  int  i)  {
                        a[i]  =  true;
                        ++i;
                }
```

```
            public static void main(String [] args) {
                    Test t = new Test();
        t.method(t.b, 0);
                    t.method(t.b, 1);
                    t.test();

                    int a = 10, b = 1;
                    a <<= b;
                    System.out.println(a);
        }
        void test() {
                    if ( b[0] && b[1] | b[2] )
                    i++;
                    if ( b[1] && b[(++i - 1)] )
                            i += 20;
                            System.out.println(i);

        }
}
Output:
22
20
```

```
161. public class Test {
        public static void main(String[] args) {
        for (byte b = Byte.MIN_VALUE; b <= Byte.MAX_VALUE;
         b++) {
            if (b == Byte.MIN_VALUE || b==Byte.MAX_VALUE)
                            System.out.println(b);
            }
        }
}
Output: Printing either -128(min) or 127(max) infinitely.
```

```
162. public class Test {
        public static void main(String[] args) {
                try {
                } finally {
                        System.out.println("First:"+
                        Long.toHexString(0x100L + 0xabcdef));
                }

                try {
                        System.exit(0);
```

```
            } finally {
                System.out.println("Second:"+
                Long.toHexString(0x100L + 0xabcdef));
            }
        }
    }
```

Output:
First:abceef

Explanation: *System.exit*(0) stops all program threads immediately. Hence, it does not execute *finally* block. The *System.exit()* used to quit program. It helps to handle shutdown in bigger programs, where all parts of the program cannot be known of each other. The shutdown hooks take care of doing all necessary shutdown ceremonies such as releasing resources, closing files etc. This method never returns back, once a thread goes there, it does not come back.

163.
```
public class Test {
        public static void main(String[] args) {
                Runtime r = Runtime.getRuntime();
                System.out.println("Max memory in MB: " +
                        r.maxMemory() / 1024);
                System.out.println("Allocated memory in MB: " +
                        r.totalMemory() / 1024);
                System.out.println("Free memory in MB: " +
                        r.freeMemory() / 1024);
                System.out.println( r.maxMemory()-r.totalMemory()
                        == r.freeMemory());
        }
}
```
Output:
Max memory in MB: 886592
Allocated memory in MB: 59776
Free memory in MB: 58837
false

164.
```
import java.math.BigDecimal;
public class Test {
        public static void main(String[] args) {
                int var1=101; float var2=(float) 100.100;
                System.out.println(var1-var2);
                System.out.println(101-100.100);
                System.out.println(new BigDecimal(var1-var2));
                System.out.println(new BigDecimal(101-var1));
        }
```

```
        }
Output:
0.9000015
0.9000000000000057
0.90000152587890625
0
```

165.
```
public class Test {
        public static void main(String[] args) {
                final int var1=1000001; final float var2=
                        (float) 10000.100;
                long l=(long) (var1*var2);
                System.out.println(var1*var2+":"+l);
        }
}
Output:  1.00001096E10:10000109568
```

166.
```
public class Test {
        public static void main(String[] args) {
                int var1=101, var2=100;
                System.out.println((var1%2==1) + ":"+(var2%2==1));
                System.out.println((var1%2!=0) + ":"+((var1&1)!=1)+
                        ":"+((var2&1)!=1));
        }
}
Output:
true:false
true:false:true
```

167.
```
public class Test {
        public static void main(String[] args) {
                System.out.println((int)(char)(byte)-1);
                System.out.println((byte)(char)(int)-1);
                System.out.println((float)(int)(byte)-1);
                System.out.println((double)(byte)(int)-1);
        }
}
Output:
65535
```

```
−1
−1.0
−1.0
```

168.
```java
public class Test {
        public static void main(String[] args) {
                Object a=123456;
                String b="0";
                System.out.println(a+=b);
        }
}
```
Output:1234560

169.
```java
public class Test {
        public static void main(String[] args) {
                Object a=123456;
                String b="0";
                System.out.println(a+=b);
            a=a+b;
                System.out.println(a+=b);
        }
}
```
Output:
1234560
123456000

170.
```java
public class Test {
        public static void main(String[] args) {
                int a='a';
                int b=1;
                System.out.println(a);
                System.out.println(a+=b);
                System.out.println((char)(a+=b));
            a=a+b;
                System.out.println(a+=b);
        }
}
```
Output:
97
```
```

98
c
101

171. ```java
public class Test {
        public static void main(String[] args) {
                int a='a';
                int b=1;
                System.out.println((char)a+b+":"+a);
        }
}
```
Output:98:97

---

172. ```java
public class Test {
        public static void main(String[] args) {
                int a='A';
                int b=1;
                System.out.println(a+'\n');
                System.out.println(a+'A');
                System.out.println(a+"A");
        }
}
```
Output:
75
130
65A

173. ```java
public class Test {
        public static void main(String[] args) {
                String a="123";
                char b[]={'A','B','C'};
                Object c=(Object)b;
                System.out.println(a+":"+b+":"+c);
        }
}
```
Output:123:[C@7926b165:[C@7926b165
```

174.
```
class Test{
     static {
            System.out.println("static block executed...");
     }
     public static void main(String[] args) {
        System.out.println("main method executed...");
     }
}
```
Output:
static block executed...
main method executed...

175.
```
public class Test {
     public static void method () {
            System.out.print("A ");
            throw new RuntimeException ();
     }
     public static void main(String [] args) {
            try {
            System.out.print("B ");
            method ();
         }
         catch (Exception re ) {
            System.out.print("C ");
         }
         finally {
            System.out.print("D ");
         }
         System.out.println("E ");
     }
}
```
Output:B A C D E

176.
```
class Test {
     public static void main(String [] args) {
        Test t = new Test ();
        t.m1();
     }
     void m1() {
        boolean b1 = false;
        boolean b2 = m(b1);
        System.out.println(b1 + " " + b2);
     }
```

```
        boolean m(boolean b1) {
            b1 = true;
            return b1;
        }
    }
    Output: False true
```

```
177. class Test {
            public void M(int i, int j) {
                    System.out.println("A="+ i+j);
            }

            public void M(int i, double j){
                    System.out.println("B="+ i+j);
            }

            public void M(double i, double j){
                    System.out.println("C="+ i+j);
            }
            public static void main(String str[]){
                    Test t = new Test();
                    t.M(1,1);
                    t.M(1,1.1);
                    t.M(1.1,1.1);
            }
    }
    Output:
    A=11
    B=11.1
    C=1.11.1
```

```
178. class Test{
        static {
                String str[]={"ABC","DEF"};
                main(str);
                System.out.println("static block executed...");
        }
        public static void main(String[] args) {
                System.out.println("main method executed..."+args[0]);
        }
    }
    Output:
```

```
            main method executed...ABC
            static block executed...
            Exception in thread "main"
            java.lang.ArrayIndexOutOfBoundsException: 0      at
              Test.main(Test.java:8)
```

Explanation: *args[0]* is not having any value since command line argument is null.

179.
```java
class Test{
    public static void main(String[] args) {
    System.out.println("a\u0024.length()+\u0024b".length());
    }
}
```
Output:
14

180.
```java
class Test{
    public static void main(String[] args) {
            char a='\n';
            char b=0X000A;
            System.out.println(a+":"+b);
    }
}
```
Output:
:

181.
```java
import java.util.Random;
class Test{
        public static void main(String[] args) {
                Random r= new Random();
                switch(r.nextInt(3)){
                case 1:
                        System.out.println("Hi");
                case 2:
                        System.out.println("Hello");
                case 3:
                        System.out.println("Bye");
                default:
                        System.out.println("Good Night");
                }
```

```
            }
        }
    Output:Good Night (output is uncertain).
```

```
182. class Test{
         public static void main(String[] args) {
                    int a=0;
                    int c=100;
                    int d=0;
                    int e=100;

                    for(int b=0;b<100;b++)   {
                             a=a++; c--; d=++d; e=--e;
                    }
             System.out.println(a+":"+c+":"+d+":"+e);
             }
     }
     Output:0:0:100:0
```

Explanation: ++ and -- does assignment of value, post increment and decrement operation respectively.

```
183. class Test{
             public static void main(String[] args) {
                  boolean i=true, j=false;
                  if( i  ) {
                                 System.out.println("1");
                         }
             else if(i && j) {
                      System.out.println( "1 && 2");
                              }
             else {
                     if ( !j ) {
                     System.out.println( "1") ;
                     }
                     else {
                         System.out.println( "2" ) ;
                             }
                 }
             }
     }
     Output:1
```

184.
```java
class Test{
    public static void main(String[] args) {
        float j=2;
        switch((int)j) {
                        default:
            System.out.println("hi");
        }
    }
}
```
Output:Hi

185.
```java
class Test {
    public static void main(String [] args) {
        Test t = new Test();
        t.m1();
    }

    void m1() {
        String str1 = "A";
        String str2 = m(str1);
        System.out.println(str1 + " " + str2);
    }

    String m(String str) {
        str = str + "B";
        System.out.print(str + " ");
        return "C";
    }
}
```
Output: AB A C

186.
```java
class Test{
    public static void main(String[] args) {
        int j=1;
        if(j) {
            System.out.println("hi");
        }
        while(j) {
            System.out.println("hi");
```

```
        }
      }
  }
Output:
Main.java:4: error: incompatible types
if(j) {
  required: boolean
  found:    int
Main.java:7: error: incompatible types
while(j) {
  required: boolean
  found:    int
```

Explanation: For condition evaluation, we require a boolean expression/value, but we are evaluating *j* which is not having a boolean value.

187.
```
class Test{
        public static int a;
    public static int M(int x) {
        System.out.print("M ");
        a = x;
        return x;
    }
    public static int N(int z) {
        System.out.print("N ");
        return a = z;
    }
    public static void main(String [] args ) {
        int b = 0;
        assert b > 0 : N(7);
        assert b > 1 : M(8);
        System.out.println("O ");
    }
}
Output:O
```

188.
```
class Test {
    public static void main(String [] args) {
        Test p = new Test();
        p.method();
    }
    void  method() {
        long [] a = {20,30,40};
        long [] b = m(a);
```

```
            System.out.print(a[0] + a[1] + a[2] + " ");
            System.out.println(b[0] + b[1] + b[2]);
        }

    long [] m(long [] c) {
        c[1] = 10;
        return c;
    }
}
```
Output:70 70

189.
```
class Test {
    public static void main(String [] args) {
        int a = 0x80000000;
        System.out.print(a);
        a =a >>> 31;
        System.out.println(a);
        int i = 100;
        double c = 100.1;
        boolean d = (i == c);
        System.out.println(d);
    }
}
```
Output:
−21474836481
false

190.
```
public class Test {
    public static void main(String [] args) {
        try {
            method();
            System.out.print("A");
        }
        catch (Exception ex) {
            System.out.print("B");
        }
        finally {
            System.out.print("C");
        }
        System.out.print("D");
    }
    public static void method() {
        throw new Error();
```

```
        }
    }
Output:
Exception in thread "main" java.lang.Error
        at Test.method(Test.java:16)
        at Test.main(Test.java:4)
```

Explanation: An exception is thrown from a method.

191.
```java
public class Test {
    public static void main(String [] args) {
        try {
            method();
            System.out.print(" 1");
        }
        catch (RuntimeException ex) {
            System.out.print(" 2");
        }
        catch (Exception ex1) {
            System.out.print(" 3");
        }
        finally {
            System.out.print(" 4");
        }
        System.out.print(" 5");
    }
    public static void method() {
        throw new RuntimeException();
    }
}
Output:2  4  5
```

192.
```java
class Test {
    public static void main(String args[]) {
        Test h = new Test();
        System.out.println(h.method());
    }
    Object method() {
        Object o = new Object();
        Object [] obj2 = new Object[1];
        obj2[0] = o;
        o = null;
        return obj2[0];
    }
}
```

```
    }
Output: java.lang.Object address.
```

```
193. class A { }
     class Test {
         A method() {
             A b = new A();
             return b;
         }
         public static void main (String args[]) {
             Test t = new Test();
             A a = t.method();
             System.out.println("a");
             a = new A();
             System.out.println("b");
         }
     }
Output:
A
B
```

```
194. public class Test {
         public static void main(String[] args) {
             try {
                         int y = 0 / 0; ;
             }
             catch(Exception e) {
                   e.printStackTrace();
             }
             finally {
                 System.out.println( "A" );
             }
         }
     }
Output:
java.lang.ArithmeticException: / by zero
         at Test.main(Test.java:7)

A
```

```
195. public class Test {
        public static void main(String [] args) {
            Boolean a = new Boolean("true");
            boolean b;
            b = a.booleanValue();
            if (!b) {
                b = true;
                System.out.print("1");
            }
            if (a & b) {
                System.out.print("2");
            }
            System.out.println("3");
        }
    }
    Output:23
```

```
196. class Test {
        public static void main(String [] args) {
            Test s = new Test();
            s.s();
        }

        void s() {
            int i = 5;
            int j = 8;
            System.out.print(" " + 2 + 4 + " ");
            System.out.print(i + j);
            System.out.print(" " + i + j + " ");
            System.out.print(m() + i + j + " ");
            System.out.println(i + j + m());
        }

        String m() {
            return "Hi";
        }
    }
    Output:24 13 58 Hi58 13Hi
```

```
197. class Test {
        boolean [] a = new boolean[13];
        int c = 0;
```

```java
    void set(boolean [] x, int i) {
        x[i] = true;
        ++c;
    }

    public static void main(String [] args) {
        Test ba = new Test();
        ba.set(ba.a, 1);
        ba.set(ba.a, 2);
        ba.m();
    }

    void m() {
        if ( a[0] && a[1] | a[2] )
            c++;
        if ( a[1] && a[(++c - 2)] )
            c += 7;
        System.out.println("c = " + c);
    }
}
Output:c = 10
```

```java
198. class Test implements Runnable {
        int a, b;
        public void run() {
            for(int i = 0; i < 1000; i++)
                synchronized(this) {
                    a = 1;
                    b = 2;
                }
            System.out.print(a + " " + b + " ");
        }
        public static void main(String args[]) {
            Test run = new Test();
            Thread t1 = new Thread(run);
            Thread t2 = new Thread(run);
            t1.start();
            t2.start();
        }
    }
Output:1  2  1  2
```

```
199. public class Test {
         public static int b;
         public static int m(int a) {
                      System.out.print("A ");
             return  b = a;
         }
         public static int n(int z) {
             System.out.print("B ");
             return b = z;
         }
         public static void main(String [] args ) {
             int  t = 0;
             assert  t > 0 : n(7);
             assert  t > 1 : m(8);
             System.out.println("C ");
         }
     }
     Output:C
```

```
200. public class Test {
         public static int a;
         public static int m(int b) {
             return b * 1;
         }
         public static void main(String [] args) {
             int  c = 2;
             assert  c > 0;
             assert  c > 1: m(c);
             if ( c < 5 )
                 assert  c > 4;

             switch (c) {
                 case 4: System.out.println("A");
                 case 5: System.out.println("B");
                 default: assert c < 6;
             }

             if ( c < 6 )
                 assert  c > 4: c++;
             System.out.println(c);
         }
     }
     Output: 2
```

```
201. public class Test {
        public static void main(String [] args) {
        String str = "12";
            try {
                str = str.concat(".1");
                double b = Double.parseDouble(str);
                str = Double.toString(b);
                int a = (int) Math.ceil(Double.valueOf(str).
                doubleValue());
                System.out.println(a);
            }
            catch (NumberFormatException e) {
                System.out.println("Exception !");
            }
        }
    }
    Output:13
```

```
202. public class Test {
        public static void stringReplace (String txt) {
            txt = txt.replace ('a' , 'b');
        }
        public static void bufferReplace (StringBuffer txt) {
            txt = txt.append ("c");
        }
        public static void main (String args[]) {
            String str = new String ("abcd");
            StringBuffer txt = new StringBuffer ("abcd");
            stringReplace(str);
            bufferReplace(txt);
            System.out.println (str + txt);
        }
    }
    Output: abcdabcdc
```

```
203. public class Test {
        public static void main(String [] args) {
            float a[ ], b[ ];
            a = new float[5];
            b = a;
            System.out.println("b[0]=" + b[0]);
        }
    }
    Output:b[0]=0.0
```

204.
```java
class A {
    byte b;
}

class Test {
    public static void main(String [] args) {
        Test p = new Test ();
        p.start ();
    }

    void start() {
        A a = new A();
        System.out.print(a.b + "  ");
        A a2 = m(a);
        System.out.println(a.b + "  " + a2.b);
    }

    A m(A tt) {
        tt.b = 11;
        return tt;
    }
}
```
Output:0 11 11

205.
```java
public class Test {
    static boolean b1, b2;
    public static void main(String [] args) {
        int x = 0;
        if ( !b1 )        {
            if ( !b2 ) {
                b1 = true;
                x++;
                if ( 1 > 2 ) {
                    x++;
                }
                if ( !b1 )
                    x = x + 2;
                else if ( b2 = true )
                    x = x + 1;
                else if ( b1 | b2 )
                    x = x + 2;
            }
        }
```

```
            System.out.println(x);
        }
    }
    Output:2
```

```
206. public class Test {
        static boolean a;
        public static void main(String [] args) {
            short s = 11;
            if ( s < 11 && !a )
                s++;
            if ( s > 11 );
            else if ( s > 10 ) {
                    s += 2;
                    s++;
                    }
                else
                --s;
            System.out.println(s);
        }
    }
    Output:14
```

```
207. public class Test {
        public static void main(String [] args) {
            double m = -9.0;
            System.out.println( Math.sqrt(m));
            String a = ""+Math.sqrt(m);
            System.out.println(a);
            a = a.substring(0,1);
            char b = a.charAt(0);
            a = a + b;
            System.out.println(a);
        }
    }
    Output:
    NaN
    NaN
    NN
```

```
208. public class Test {
        public static void main(String [] args) {
            int r = 0;

            Boolean bool1 = new Boolean("TRUE");
            Boolean bool2 = new Boolean("true");
            Boolean bool3 = new Boolean("tRuE");
            Boolean bool4 = new Boolean("false");

            if (bool1 == bool2)
                r = 1;
            if (bool1.equals(bool2) )
                r = r + 1;
            if (bool2 == bool4)
                r = r + 10;
            if (bool2.equals(bool4) )
                r = r + 100;
            if (bool2.equals(bool3) )
                r = r + 1000;
            System.out.println("r = " + r);
        }
    }
    Output: r = 1001
```

```
209. class Test extends Thread {
        final StringBuffer s1 = new StringBuffer();
        final StringBuffer s2 = new StringBuffer();

        public static void main(String args[]) {
            final Test t = new Test();

            new Thread() {
                public void run() {
                    synchronized(this) {
                        t.s1.append("1");
                        t.s2.append("2");
                        System.out.println(t.s1);
                        System.out.println(t.s2);
                    }
                }
            }.start();

            new Thread() {
                public void run() {
                    synchronized(this)                          {
                        t.s1.append("3");
```

```
                        t.s2.append("4");
                        System.out.println(t.s2);
                        System.out.println(t.s1);
                    }
                }
            }.start();
        }
    }
    Output:
    1
    2
    24
    13
```

```
210. class Test extends Thread {
         public static void main(String [] args) {
             Test t = new Test();
             Thread a = new Thread(t);
             a.start();
         }
         public void run() {
             for(int i = 0; i < 2; ++i) {
                 System.out.println(i);
             }
         }
     }
     Output:
     0
     1
```

```
211. public class Test {
         public static void main(String [] args ) {
             int r = 0;
             Test t = new Test();
             Object o = t;

             if (o == t)
                 r = 1;
             if (o != t)
                 r = r + 1;
             if (o.equals(t) )
                 r = r + 10;
             if (t.equals(o) )
```

```
            r = r + 100;
        System.out.println("r = " + r);
    }
}
Output: r = 111
```

```
212. public class Test {
        public static void main(String[] args) {
            String str = "foo";
            Object obj = (Object)str;
            if (str.equals(obj)) {
                System.out.print("1");
            }
            else {
                System.out.print("2");
            }
            if (obj.equals(str)) {
                System.out.print("3");
            }
            else {
                System.out.print("4");
            }
        }
}
Output:13
```

```
213. public class Test {
        static int q;
        static void m(int p) {
            boolean a;
            do {
                a = p<10 | m1(1);
                a = p<10 || m1(2);
            }while (!a);
        }
        static boolean m1(int p) {
            q += p;
            return true;
        }
        public static void main(String[] args) {
            m(0);
            System.out.println( "q = " + q );
        }
```

```
        }
        Output:q = 1
```

```
214. public class Test {
         public static void main (String [] args) {
             Thread th = new Thread() {
                 Clz m = new Clz();
                 public void run() {
                     System.out.println( m.method(22));
                 }
             };
         th.start();
         }
     }
     class Clz {
         private int d = 11;
         public int method(int a) {
             int x = d;
             return d = x + a;
         }
     }
     Output:33
```

```
215. class A { }
     class B extends A { }
     class C extends A { }
     public class Test {
         public static void main (String [] args) {
             A a = new B();
             if( a instanceof B )
                 System.out.println ("B");
             else if( a instanceof A )
                 System.out.println ("A");
             else if( a instanceof C )
                 System.out.println ( "C" );
             else
                 System.out.println ("D ");
         }
     }
     Output:B
```

216. ```java
class A extends Exception { }
class B extends A { }
public class Test {
    public static void main(String args[]) {
        try {
            throw new B();
        }
        catch (A a) {
            System.out.println("A");
        }
        catch (Exception e) {
            System.out.println("B");
        }
    }
}
```
Output:B

---

217. ```java
public abstract class Test
{
    public int method()
    {
        return 22;
    }
    public abstract class B
    {
        public int method()
        {
            return 33;
        }
    }
    public static void main (String [] args) {
        Test t = new Test() {
            public int method() {
                return 44;
            }
        };
        Test.B b = t.new B() {
            public int method() {
                return 55;
            }
        };

        System.out.println(b.method() + " " + t.method());
    }
}
```
Output:55 44

218.
```java
public class Test implements Runnable
{
    private int a;
    private int b;

    public static void main(String [] args) {
        Test t = new Test();
        (new Thread(t)).start( );
        (new Thread(t)).start( );
    }
    public synchronized void run( ) {
        for (;;) {
            a++;
            b++;
            System.out.println("a = " + a + " b = " + b);
            if(a==b)
                break;
        }
    }
}
```
Output:
```
a = 1 b = 1
a = 2 b = 2
```

219.
```java
class Test extends Thread {
    public static void main(String [] args) {
        Test t = new Test();
        t.run();
    }

    public void run() {
        for(int i=1; i < 5; ++i) {
            System.out.print((i!=i) + " ");
        }
    }
}
```
Output: false false false false

```
220. public class Test extends Thread {
         public void run() {
             System.out.println("A");
             yield();
             System.out.println("B");
         }
         public static void main(String []argv) {
             (new Test()).start();
         }
     }
     Output:
     A
     B
```

```
221. public class Test implements Runnable {
         private int a;
         private int b;

         public static void main(String args[]) {
             Test t = new Test();
             (new Thread(t)).start();
             (new Thread(t)).start();
         }
         public synchronized void run() {
             for(int i = 0; i < 4; i++) {
                 a++;
                 b++;
                 System.out.println("a = " + a + ", b = " + b);
             }
         }
     }
     Output:
     a = 1, b = 1
     a = 2, b = 2
     a = 3, b = 3
     a = 4, b = 4
     a = 5, b = 5
     a = 6, b = 6
     a = 7, b = 7
     a = 8, b = 8
```

```
222. public class Test {
         public static void main(String [] args) {
```

```
                    int  r  =  0;
                    short  s  =  5;
                    Long  a  =  new  Long("5");
                    Long  b  =  new  Long(5);
                    Short  c  =  new  Short("5");
                    Short  a1  =  new  Short(s);
                    Integer  b1  =  new  Integer("5");
                    Integer  c1  =  new  Integer(5);
                    if  (a  ==  b)
                        r  =  1;
                    if  (a.equals(b)  )
                        r  =  r  +  1;
                    if  (a.equals(c)  )
                        r  =  r  +  10;
                    if  (a.equals(a1)  )
                        r  =  r  +  100;
                    if  (a.equals(c1)  )
                        r  =  r  +  1000;
                    System.out.println("r  =  "  +  r);
                }
            }
        Output:  r  =  1
```

```
223. class  Test  {
        public  static  void  main(String[]  args)  {
            int  a  =  1;
            int  b  =  2;
            String  str  =  "A";
            System.out.println(a  +  b  +  str);
            String  str1  =  "ABC";
            String  str2  =  "DEF";
            String  str3  =  str2;
            str2  =  "GHI";
            System.out.println(str1  +  str2  +  str3);
        }
    }
    Output:
    3A
    ABCGHIDEF
```

```
224. class  A  {
        A()  {
            System.out.print("A");
```

```
        }
    }
    public class Test extends A {
        public static void main(String [] args) {
            new Test();
            new A();
        }
    }
    Output:AA
```

```
225. public class Test extends A {
         public static void main(String [] args) {
             Test t = new Test();
             t.method();
         }
     }
     abstract class A {
         void method() {
             for (int a = 0; a < 5; a++,a++ ) {
                 System.out.print(" " + a);
             }
         }
     }
     Output:0 2 4
```

```
226. import java.util.Vector;
     class A extends Vector {
         int i = 1;
         public int ABC() {
             return (i=2)*i++;
         }
     }
     public class Test extends A {
         public Test () {
             i = 3;
         }
         public static void main (String args []) {
             A a = new Test();
             System.out.println(a.ABC());
         }
     }
     Output:4
```

227.
```java
public class Test {
    public int m() {
        static int j = 0;
        j++;
        return j;
    }
    public static void main(String args[]) {
        Test t = new Test();
        t.m();
        int k = t.m();
        System.out.println(k);
    }
}
```
Output:
Main.java:3: error: illegal start of expression
        static int j = 0;

Explanation: Static variables are defined at class level. It cannot be declared inside a method.

228.
```java
public class Test {
    public static void main(String args[]){
        try {
            Float a = new Float("5.0");
            byte b = a.byteValue();
            int c = a.intValue();
            double d = a.doubleValue();
            System.out.println(c + b + d);
        }
        catch (NumberFormatException e) {
            System.out.println("Exception");
        }
    }
}
```
Output:15.0

229.
```java
public class Test {
    public static void main(String[] args) {
        String str = "Hi";
        Object obj = str;
        String str2= new String("Hi");
```

```
        if ( obj.equals(str) )    {
            System.out.println("A");
        }
        else {
            System.out.println("B");
        }
        if ( str.equals(obj) )    {
            System.out.println("C");
        }
        else  {
            System.out.println("D");
        }
        if ( str2==str  ) {
            System.out.println("A");
        }
        else {
            System.out.println("B");
        }
        if ( obj==str  ) {
            System.out.println("C");
        }
        else  {
            System.out.println("D");
        }
    }
}
Output:
A
C
B
C
```

---

230. Write a sorting program of non-zero array elements with using != operator and exchanges elements without using temporary variable.

```
    import java.util.*;
import java.lang.*;
import java.io.*;
class Test{
public static void main(String args[])
{
int i,j,n=5;
int a[] = {12,34,44,3,5};
for(j=0;(n-j)!= 0 ?true:false;j++)
for(i=j+1;(n-i)!=0?true:false;i++)
if((a[i]/a[j]!=0)?true:false)
{
```

```
a[i] =a[i] + a[j];
a[j] =a[i] - a[j];
a[i] =a[i] - a[j];
}
for(i=0;i<n;i++)
System.out.println(a[i]+",");

}
}
```
Output:
44,34,12,5,3

Explanation: In this program, the conditions are, not to use ==,<,>,<=,>= and do-not use temporary variable for exchanging elements position. Both outer and inner *for* loop uses != and ?: operators for condition checking. Condition *a[i]/a[j]!=0* checks weather number is bigger/smaller.

231.
```
import java.util.logging.Level;
import java.util.logging.Logger;
class Test {
    private volatile boolean flag = false;
    public static void main(String args[]) throws InterruptedException {
        final Test test = new Test();

        Runnable task = new Runnable(){

            @Override
            public void run(){
                try {
                    test.method1();
                } catch (InterruptedException ex) {
                    Logger.getLogger(Test.class.getName()).
                        log(Level.SEVERE, null, ex);
                }
            System.out.println(Thread.currentThread()
            + " finished Execution");
            }
        };

        Runnable notifyTask = new Runnable(){

            @Override
            public void run(){
                test.method2();
            System.out.println(Thread.currentThread()
            + " finished Execution");
            }
        };
```

```
        Thread t1 = new Thread(task, "WT1"); //will wait
        Thread t2 = new Thread(task, "WT2"); //will wait
        Thread t3 = new Thread(task, "WT3"); //will wait
        Thread t4 = new Thread(notifyTask,"NT1"); //will notify

        //starting all waiting thread
        t1.start();
        t2.start();
        t3.start();

        //pause to ensure all waiting thread started successfully
        Thread.sleep(200);

        //starting notifying thread
        t4.start();

    }
    private synchronized void method1() throws InterruptedException
    {
        while(flag != true){
            System.out.println(Thread.currentThread()
                        + " wait on this object");
            wait(); //release lock and reacquires on wakeup
        System.out.println(Thread.currentThread() + " is woken up");
        }
        flag = false; //resetting condition
    }

    private synchronized void method2() {
        while (flag == false){
            System.out.println(Thread.currentThread()
            + " notify all or one thread waiting on this object");

        flag = true; //making condition true for waiting thread
            //notify(); // only one out of three waiting thread
                                //WT1, WT2,WT3 will woke up
        notifyAll(); // all waiting thread WT1, WT2,WT3 will woke up
        }

    }

}
Output:
Thread[WT1,5,main] wait on this object
Thread[WT2,5,main] wait on this object
Thread[WT3,5,main] wait on this object
Thread[NT1,5,main] notify all or one thread waiting on this object
Thread[NT1,5,main] finished Execution
Thread[WT3,5,main] is woken up
```

```
Thread[WT2,5,main]  is  woken  up
Thread[WT2,5,main]  wait  on  this  object
Thread[WT1,5,main]  is  woken  up
Thread[WT1,5,main]  wait  on  this  object
Thread[WT3,5,main]  finished  Execution
```

Explanation: The program shows how all threads gets notified if we call *notifyAll* method but just one Thread will wake up if we call *notify* method. This program has three threads which will wait if boolean variable *flag* is false, here boolean *flag* is a volatile variable, hence all threads can have its updated value. Starting three threads WT1, WT2, WT3 will wait as variable *flag* is *false* than one thread NT1 will make *flag true*. A *notify* call gives no guarantee which thread will woke up. A *notifyAll* will wake up all threads, they will compete for monitor/lock and the Thread which will get the lock first will finish its execution and resetting *flag* to *false*. This will force other two threads remain waiting. This program will not exit because other two threads are still waiting and they are not daemon threads.

---

232. Write a program to sort only even numbers in a array, odd number position remain same, example: 23, 20, 1, 90, 10, 4, 3 and result array should look like: 23, 4, 1, 10, 20, 90, 3.

```java
class Test{
static boolean change(int num[], int index)
{
int min=9999999, f=index;
for(int i=index;i<7; i++)
{
if(num[i]%2 == 0 && num[i]<min){
min=num[i];
f=i;
}
}
//exchange
int t=num[index];
num[index]=min;
num[f]=t;
return true;
}
  public static void main(String arg[]){
    int[] num={23, 20, 1, 90, 10, 4, 3};
    for(int i=0; i< 7; i++){
    if(num[i]%2==0)
    change(num, i);
    System.out.println(num[i]+",");
    }
  }
}
Output:
 23, 4, 1, 10, 20, 90, 3
```

Explanation: Sort the even numbers by maintaining odd number's position, in the *main* method identifies even number and makes a call to *change* function to find the smallest number and exchange with other number, repeats until array completes.

---

233. In a String array, find a characters set which will form a word out of last character of different Strings. List the matched strings. Example: Find "tea" characters in the array: Cat,Top,Hat,Tree,Home,Shirt,Book,Zebra. So matches Hat, Tree and Zebra.

```
class Test{
public static void main(String str1[])
{
String str[]= {"Cat","Top","Hat","Tree","Home","Shirt","Book","Zebra"};
for (int i=0; i<8;i++)
{
System.out.println("tea".indexOf(str[i].substring(str[i].length()
 - 1)) >=0? str[i]:"");
}
}
}
Output:
Cat
Hat
Tree
Home
Shirt
Zebra
```

Explanation: All built in functions of *String* used to find the required strings.

---

234. Write a program to create deadlock between two threads.

```
class Test {
    String s1 = "Chandrakant";
    String s2 = "Vaishnavi";

    Thread t1 = new Thread("Thread 1"){
        public void run(){
            while(true){
                synchronized(s1){
                    synchronized(s2){
                        System.out.println(s1 + s2);
                    }
                }
            }
        }
    };
```

```
        Thread  t2  =  new  Thread("Thread  2"){
            public  void  run(){
                while(true){
                    synchronized(s2){
                        synchronized(s1){
                            System.out.println(s2  +  s1);
                        }
                    }
                }
            }
        };

        public  static  void  main(String  a[]){
            Test  t  =  new  Test();
            t.t1.start();
            t.t2.start();
        }
    }
}
```

Output:
ChandrakantVaishnavi
;
:
:

---

235. Reverse a number.

```
class  Test  {
    public  int  method(int  number){

        int  reverse  =  0;
        while(number  !=  0){
            reverse  =  (reverse*10)+(number%10);
            number  =  number/10;
        }
        return  reverse;
    }

    public  static  void  main(String  a[]){
        Test  t  =  new  Test();
        System.out.println("Reverse: "+t.method(12345));
    }
}
```

Output:
54321

236. Reverse a string using recursion.

```java
class Test {
    String reverse = "";
    public String method(String str){
        if(str.length() == 1){
            return str;
        } else {
            reverse += str.charAt(str.length()-1)
                    +method(str.substring(0,str.length()-1));
            return reverse;
        }
    }

    public static void main(String a[]){
        Test t = new Test();
        System.out.println("Result: "+t.method("Chandrakant"));
    }
}
```
Output:
tnakardnahC

---

237. Find duplicate characters in a string.

```java
import java.util.HashMap;
import java.util.Map;
import java.util.Set;
public class Test {
    public void method(String str){
        Map<Character, Integer> mp = new HashMap<Character, Integer>();
        char[] chrs = str.toCharArray();
        for(Character ch:chrs){
            if(mp.containsKey(ch)){
                mp.put(ch, mp.get(ch)+1);
            } else {
                mp.put(ch, 1);
            }
        }
        Set<Character> keys = mp.keySet();
        for(Character ch:keys){
            if(mp.get(ch) > 1){
                System.out.println(ch+"=>"+mp.get(ch));
            }
        }
    }

    public static void main(String a[]){
        Test t = new Test();
```

```
            t.method("Chandrakant");
      }
}
Output:
a=>3
n=>2
```

238. Find top two maximum numbers in a array.

```
class Test {
    public void method(int[] nums){
        int maxOne = 0;
        int maxTwo = 0;
        for(int n:nums){
            if(maxOne < n){
                maxTwo = maxOne;
                maxOne =n;
            } else if(maxTwo < n){
                maxTwo = n;
            }
        }
        System.out.println("First Max Number: "+maxOne);
        System.out.println("Second Max Number: "+maxTwo);
    }

    public static void main(String a[]){
        int n[] = {13,54,67,42,4,12,9,88};
        Test t = new Test();
        t.method(n);
    }
}
Output:
First Max Number: 88
Second Max Number: 67
```

239. Find the sum of digits of a number.

```
public class Test {
        int sum = 0;
        public int method(int number){

                if(number == 0){
                        return sum;
                } else {
```

```
                        sum += (number%10);
                        method(number/10);
                }
                return sum;
        }

        public static void main(String a[]){
                Test t = new Test();
                System.out.println("Sum: "+t.method(123));
        }
}
```
Output:
Sum:6

---

240. Find longest substring without repeating characters.

```java
import java.util.HashSet;
import java.util.Set;
class Test {
    private Set<String> subStrList = new HashSet<String>();
    private int finalSubStrSize = 0;
    public Set<String> method(String input){
        //reset instance variables
        subStrList.clear();
        finalSubStrSize = 0;
        // have a boolean flag on each character ascii value
        boolean[] flag = new boolean[256];
        int j = 0;
        char[] inputCharArr = input.toCharArray();
        for (int i = 0; i < inputCharArr.length; i++) {
            char c = inputCharArr[i];
            if (flag[c]) {
                subStr(inputCharArr,j,i);
                for (int k = j; k < i; k++) {
                    if (inputCharArr[k] == c) {
                        j = k + 1;
                        break;
                    }
                    flag[inputCharArr[k]] = false;
                }
            } else {
                flag[c] = true;
            }
        }
        subStr(inputCharArr,j,inputCharArr.length);
        return subStrList;
    }
```

```
    private String subStr(char[] inputArr, int start, int end)
          {
        StringBuilder sb = new StringBuilder();
        for(int i=start;i<end;i++){
            sb.append(inputArr[i]);
        }
        String subStr = sb.toString();
        if(subStr.length() > finalSubStrSize){
            finalSubStrSize = subStr.length();
            subStrList.clear();
            subStrList.add(subStr);
        } else if(subStr.length() == finalSubStrSize){
            subStrList.add(subStr);
        }

        return sb.toString();
    }

    public static void main(String a[]){
        Test t = new Test();
        System.out.println(t.method("Chandrakant"));
        System.out.println(t.method("Chandra_Chandra_Chandra"));
        System.out.println(t.method("abcdefgh"));
        System.out.println(t.method("11223344"));
    }
}
Output:
[Chandr]
[ndra_Ch, _Chandr]
[abcdefgh]
[23, 34, 12]
```

241. Check the given number is binary number or not?

```
class Test {
    public boolean method(int binary){
        boolean status = true;
        while(true){
            if(binary == 0){
                break;
            } else {
                int tmp = binary%10;
                if(tmp > 1){
                    status = false;
                    break;
                }
```

```
                binary = binary/10;
            }
        }
        return status;
    }

    public static void main(String a[]){
        Test t = new Test();
        System.out.println("Is 1110101 binary? :"+t.method(1110101));
        System.out.println("Is 0011002 binary? :"+t.method(0011002));
    }
}
```
Output:
Is 1110101 binary? :true
Is 0011002 binary? :false

---

242. Convert binary to decimal number.

```
class Test {
    public int method(int binary){
        int decimal = 0;
        int power = 0;
        while(true){
            if(binary == 0){
                break;
            } else {
                int tmp = binary%10;
                decimal += tmp*Math.pow(2, power);
                binary = binary/10;
                power++;
            }
        }
        return decimal;
    }

    public static void main(String a[]){
        Test t = new Test();
        System.out.println("1001 : "+t.method(1001));
        System.out.println("1101 : "+t.method(1101));
    }
}
```
Output:
1001 : 9
1101 : 13

243. Find the sum of the first 1000 prime numbers.

```java
class Test {
    public static void main(String args[]){
        int number = 2;
        int count = 0;
        long sum = 0;
        while(count < 1000){
            if(method(number)){
                sum += number;
                count++;
            }
            number++;
        }
        System.out.println(sum);
    }

    private static boolean method(int number){
        for(int i=2; i<=number/2; i++){
            if(number % i == 0){
                return false;
            }
        }
        return true;
    }
}
```
Output:
3682913

244. Find Two Largest Numbers from Integer Array

```java
import java.util.Arrays;
class Test{
    static int big1 = Integer.MIN_VALUE;
    static int big2 = Integer.MIN_VALUE;
    public static void main(String args[]) {
        max(new int[]{100, 22, 567, 12, 690});
    }

    public static void max( int[] numbers) {
        for (int number : numbers) {
            if (number > big1) {
                big2 = big1;
                big1 = number;
            } else if (number > big2) {
                big2 = number;
            }
        }
```

```
                System.out.println("Unsorted array is : " +
                Arrays.toString(numbers));
                System.out.println("First maximum  is : " + big1);
                System.out.println("Second maximum  is : " + big2);
            }

        }
```

Output:
Unsorted array is : [100, 22, 567, 12, 690]
First maximum is : 690
Second maximum is : 567

---

245. Programming Exercises

(i) Write a program to this logic. There is a array-A with element's sum=X1 and elements size=N1, we have to form a array-B with size N1(array-A's size) such that it's element's sum=X1(array-A's sum) and conditions are: no duplicates allowed and should not match any elements in the array-A.
Example: Input: Array-A=11,12,13,15 = 51
Output: 10,14,18,9 =51
Hint: Either increase/decrease for two elements each time of iteration to balance the sum.
Note:All arrays need not have solution.

(ii) Sort an array without using relationship operators and exchange elements without using temporary variables, use logical operators only to exchange variables.
Hint: This program is partially solved in the previous exercises.

(iii) Sort an array with using array's first element only.
Example: Input: Array-A=15,11,20,75
Output:Array-A=75,20,15,11
Hint: Array-A=15,11,20,75 use first element which is 15, then intermediate array is 0,4,-5,-60, sort it and save it's indexes for next level, we get -60,-5,0,4, bring original elements using indexes which is Array-A=75,20,15,11.

(iv) How to check weather an array is sorted or not in O(n/2)?
Hint: try if(!a[i] <= a[i+1] && a[n-i] >= a[n-i-1])

(v) Find the minimum differences between 2 array's elements such that first element comes first and second element comes next.
Input: a[10,9,18,29]
Output:10-9=1
Hint: In the above array, we can find difference like this, 10-9=1, 10-18=-8, 10-29=-19 and 9-29=-20, so here 1 is the minimum difference not -20.

(vi) Write a program to check weather a number is odd or not, if odd then find that number is prime or not?

(vii) Select odd position characters in a String using recursive function.
Input:Chandrakant
Output:Cadaat
Hint: In the recursive method check odd index characters.

(viii) Find first and last non repeated characters of a given String?
Input:Chandrakant
Output:Ct

(ix) Find all pairs in an array of integers whose sum is equal to other pair's sum.
Input:10,30,25,15
Output:10+30=40 and 25+15=40

(x) Find three largest numbers of a array.

(xi) Add two integer without using arithmetic operators.

(xii) Reverse a integer number and check weather it is a palindrome or not.

(xiii) Find substrings of size N from a String.
Input: Str=Bangalore
Input Size=4
Output: Bang, anga,ngal, galo, alor,lore....

(xiv) Reverse two halves of a string and construct a string. Write a program to evaluate this.
Input:ABCDEFGH
Output:DCBAHGFE

(xv) There are two arrays, one array has base numbers which is sorted in ascending order, other array has all number's powers, identify which base has to get which power. Write a program to evaluate above logic.
Input: Array-A=1,2,3 and Array-B=2,8,3
Output:$1^8, 2^3, 3^2$

(xvi) Write a program to evaluate this problem, one array has numbers and another array has it's sum of digits, identify which number matches which digits sum.
Input: Array-A=234,123,567 and Array-B=6,9,18
Output:234=9, 123=6 and 567=18

(xvii) Write a program to evaluate this problem, there are three arrays, one has unsorted strings which is used to form a sentence, second and third arrays has partial sorted elements, first array's string positions are mentioned in the second array, if a pair of numbers in second and third arrays appears more than twice, then that can be considered for final sorting, based on this analysis, correlate one-to-one match with first array, rearrange the array-one such that it forms a correct sentence.
Input:Array-1=a Java book This is, Array-2=3,4,5,1,2 and Array-3=1,2,3,4,5
Output:This is a Java book (positions: 1,2,3,4,5)

(xviii) Check weather key is existed or not in an array of numbers in O(n/4).
Hint: Have multiple conditions check in a *if* statement in n/4 *for* loop. Similar to this a[i]==key || a[i/2+1]==key || a[n/2-i]==key || a[n-i-1]==key....

(xix) Write a program to evaluate this problem, there is a array of numbers, few numbers are big and few are small, make sure that all numbers are having same number of digits by adding/subtracting from array of numbers.
Input: 1000, 2000, 300, 900
Output:1000, 1000, 1200, 1000 (there could be other possibilities)

(xx) Write a program to evaluate this problem, in a strings of array, except two strings rest of them are duplicates, find non-unique numbers.
Input: ABC, ABC, CDE, EFG, ABC
Output: CDE and EFG

(xxi) Write a program to evaluate this problem, in a array of numbers, sum of last four digits of numbers should be 10.
Input:11045, 12345, 450631
Output: 11045 and 450631

(xxii) Write a program to evaluate this problem, multiply 2 numbers without using */+, use only recursion technique.
Hint: Use logical operators.

(xxiii) Find a number in a string.
Hint: Use ASCII checking/digits checking technique.

(xxiv) Achieve operator overloading similar to C++ in Java.
Hint: Operators should be passed as argument to function in a string, function should have switch to evaluate all operators.

(xxv) Count the number of lines, words, characters, of the same writing program using *File* technique.

(xxvi) Compute m^n (m power n) without using the * and without using library functions.

(xxvii) Exchange the first half array elements with second half array elements without using temporary variable.

(xxviii) Divide each element of array by the last element of the array using recursive function.

(xxix) Sum of all diagonal elements of 2D matrix using recursion technique.

(xxx) Migrate 2D array elements into 1D array elements using recursive function.

(xxxi) Compute the factorial of the given number without using * and use recursive function only.

(xxxii) Find the number of occurrences of each character in a given string.

Chapter 4

Important Concepts

1. Threads can be created either by extending the *Thread* class or by implementing the *Runnable* interface.

2. Java Packages and its purpose:
   java.util - Data structure classes
   java.lang - Basic language functionality and fundamental types
   java.math - Multiprecision arithmetic
   java.io - File operation
   java.nio - File operation
   java.awt - Native GUI components
   javax.swing - Platform independent GUI component
   java.applet - Classes for creating an applet
   java.net - Networking operation, sockets and DNS lookups
   java.security - Key generation, encryption and decryption
   java.sql - Java database connectivity (JDBC) to access database

3. Components of JVM,

   a. Compiler - To convert high level language program into bytecode.

   b. Editor - Used to edit the Java program.

   c. Loader - To load the files from secondary storage device like hard disk, flash drive, compact disk into RAM for execution. It also loads class files.

   d. Linker - It combines all refereed program files from various places into the main program.

   e. Execution - Actual execution of the native code, which is handled by OS.

4. Translator is a program that converts Java program into native machine language. There are of three types of translators: (i) *Interpreter* converts line by line of bytecode into native machine code, (ii) *Compiler* reads all lines and convert all lines into native code, and (iii) *Assembler* is used for transform assembly level language into machine level language.

5. Backslash character constants and their meaning,

Character	Meaning
\b	Back space
\f	Form feed

\n	New line
\r	Carriage return
\t	Horizontal tab
\'	Single quote
\"	Double quote
\\	Backslash

6. Compared to C, execution of Java is slow because linking is done at run-time. Every time the program is executed in Java the conversion of bytecode into native machine code is done at run-time, this overhead reduces the speed of execution.

7. Enums restricts a variable to have only a few predefined values. The values in this enumerated list are called *enums*.

8. Java class loaders are hierarchical. The classes loaded by a child class loader have visibility into classes loaded by its parents. However, the reverse is not true.

9. Stream represents flow of data from one place to another place. There are three different streams and their functions are as follows, (i) *System.out* displays output on monitor, (ii)*System.in* receives data from keyboard/input device and (iii) *System.err* used to output error message.

10. Java does not support multiple inheritance but supports multiple interface inheritance.

11. Static method is called and executed without using any object.

12. Code reuse can be done through inheritance.

13. Java abstraction is the process of exposing only the needed essential characteristics and behaviour with respect to a context. The interface achieves 100% abstraction and abstract class give 0-100% abstraction.

14. Java supports single line and multi-line comments. Any text/characters available inside comment are ignored by the Java compiler.

15. Encapsulation combines data and actions together. Thus restricted access to critical data members in a program improves security.

16. Default value of variables and its type,

Variable Type	Default Value
byte	0
short	0
int	0
long	0L
float	0f
double	0d
char	*null*
boolean	false
reference	*null*

17. JVM is written in C-language and Java is case sensitive.

18. *.exe* contains machine code which is understandable by the microprocessor. Further, it is system dependent

19. *.class* or bytecode is system independent. It contains bytecode instructions understandable by JVM.

20. Virus is a self replicating software. However, it will not spread from text file. Virus cannot spread from *.class* because it is text file.

21. Every word of class names and interface names start with a capital letter.

22. Exception represents runtime error. If any runtime error occurs, it does not terminate program execution.

23. Major data types in Java are primitive data types and reference/object data types.

24. Operators and its meaning:

Operator	Meaning
+	Addition or Arithmetic plus
−	Subtraction or Arithmetic minus
*	Arithmetic multiplication
/	Arithmetic division
%	Arithmetic modulo
<	Less than (Relational)
>	Greater than (Relational)
<=	Less than or equal to (Relational)
>=	Greater than or equal to (Relational)
==	Is equal to (Relational)
!=	is not equal to (Relational)
&&	Logical AND
||	Logical OR
!	Logical NOT

25. Prefer using *ArrayList* or *HashMap* compared to *Vector* or *Hashtable* to avoid any synchronization overhead. The *ArrayList* or *HashMap* can be externally synchronized for concurrent access by multiple threads.

26. *String* class is immutable. However, *StringBuffer* and *StringBuilder* classes are mutable. Hence it is more efficient to use *StringBuffer* or *StringBuilder* as compared to *String* for computation intensive situations (i.e. loops like *for, while* etc.).

27. Inheritance is a way to define a new class using classes which have already been defined. Polymorphism is the ability of methods to behave differently based on the object invoking it.

28. During program execution, message can be passed through input device using command line is known as command line arguments. Further, there is no restriction on the number of command

line arguments. Command line arguments can be used to specify configuration information while launching the application. Message is passed as *Strings* and they are captured into the *String* argument of the *main* method.

29. Java Input/Output performance can be improved using buffering, minimizing access to the underlying hard disk and operating systems. Use the *NIO* package for improving performance include non-blocking I/O operations, buffers to hold data and memory mapping of files.

30. When providing a user defined key class for storing objects in *HashMap*, needs to override *equals()*, and *hashCode()* methods from the Object class.

31. Hashcode is the unique id given to every object by the JVM. Hashcode is also known as reference number.

32. The garbage collection cannot be enforced, but you can adequately ask the garbage collector to collect garbage.

33. Wrapper classes allow primitive data types to be accessed as objects. So that they can be *serializable* e.g, *Integer, Float, Byte, Character, Long*, etc.

34. *Serialization* is a process of writing an object to a file. However, transient variables cannot be serialized.

35. Every time an object is created in Java, it goes into heap memory. The primitive variables are allocated in the stack, if they are local method variables and in the heap if they are class member variables.

36. Constructor is a special type of method that determines how an object should be initialized while creating an object. A constructor has the same name as the class and has no return value. It is always called with the *new* operator.

37. Threads are unsafe if it shares same heap spaces, and the threads which have their own stack space are safe.

38. Two types of exceptions are (i) checked (i.e. compiler checked) and (ii) unchecked (runtime Exceptions).

39. Different types of access modifiers provided in Java are as follows,
    a. Public: Declared as *public* can be accessed from anywhere.
    b. Private: Declared as *private* is not visible outside of its class.
    c. Protected: Declared as *protected* can be accessed by classes in the same package and subclasses in the other packages.
    d. Default modifier: Can be accessed only to classes in the same package.

40. The Assignment Operators and its description:

Operator	Description
=	Simple assignment operator. Assigns values from right side operands to left side operand.
+ =	Add and assignment operator. This operator adds right operand to the left operand and assign the result to left operand.
− =	Subtract and assignment operator. This operator subtracts right operand from the left operand and assign the result to left operand.
* =	Multiply and assignment operator. This operator multiplies right operand with the left operand and assign the result to left operand.
/ =	Divide and assignment operator. This operator divides left operand with the right operand and assign the result to left operand.

% =	Modulus and assignment operator. Determines modulus using two operands and assign the result to left operand.
<<=	Left shift and assignment operator.
>>=	Right shift and assignment operator.
& =	Bitwise AND and assignment operator.
∧ =	Bitwise Ex-OR and assignment operator.
| =	Bitwise inclusive OR and assignment operator.

41. JVM process is an execution of a program, but a thread is a single logical execution sequence within the process which can be created by either extending the *Thread* class or implementing the *Runnable* interface.

42. Following are different modes of memory allocation in Java for effective management,
    a. Heap - Used for objects (may also contain reference variables).
    b. Stack - Used for methods, local variables and reference variables.
    c. Static - Used for static data/methods.
    d. Code - Used for code section that contains your byte-code.

43. Creating two methods with same name with same type and arguments called method overriding. It is a super and subclass relationship. The method signature includes, method name, parameter list and return type. The overridden method can broaden the accessibility, but could not reduce it, i.e. if it is *private* in the super class, the child class can make it *public* but not vice versa.

44. Classes defined within another class is called as inner classes. An inner class has accessibility including *private*. However, anonymous is a class defined inside a method without a name, instantiated, declared in the same position and cannot have explicit constructors.

45. Variables defined within methods, constructors or blocks are called *local* variables. The variable is declared and initialized within the method and the variable will be destroyed as soon as the control leaves the method or block or constructors.

46. Instance variables are variables inside a class, but outside any method. These variables are instantiated when the class is loaded. Instance variables can be accessed by any method, constructor or blocks of that particular class.

47. Class variables are variables declared inside a class, outside any method with *static* keyword.

48. In object casting, the best practice is to incorporate the *instanceof* operator in the program. Using *instanceof*, the target object type can be verified before typecasting. This ensures that wrong cast of an object and avoids runtime errors.

49. Static polymorphism relates to method overloading whereas dynamic polymorphism relates to method overriding.

50. Java generics are one of the most contentious Java language features. Generics allow a type or method to operate on objects of different types while providing compile-time type safety, making Java an entirely statically typed language.

51. The *null* and *sizeof* are not keywords in Java.

52. About *main()* method in Java,
   a. The *main* method is entry point for any core Java program. Execution starts from *main()* method.
   b. The *main* method must be declared *public, static* and *void*. Otherwise JVM will not able to run Java program.
   c. The *main* method is run by a special thread called *"main"* thread in Java. Java program will be running until *main* thread is running or any non-daemon thread spawned from main method is running.
   d. Apart from *static, void* and *public*, you can use *synchronized, final* and *strictfp* modifier in the signature of *main* method.
   e. The *main* method can be declared using var-args syntax from Java 1.5 onwards e.g. *public static void main(String... args)*
   f. In Java, the *main* method can be overloaded like any other method, but JVM will only invoke *main* method with specified signature specified above.
   g. Static initializer block is executed even before JVM calls *main* function. It is executed when a class is loaded into memory by JVM.
   h. The *throws* clause can be used in the signature of *main* method and can throw any checked or unchecked exception.

53. The transient modifier applies to variables only and it is not stored as part of the object's persistent condition. Transient variables are not serialized.

54. *Volatile* modifier applies to variables only and it tells the compiler that the variable value can be changed unpredictably by the other parts of the program(threads can change this value).

55. The *Vector* class provides the capability to implement a re-sizable array of objects.

56. Auto boxing (Java 5 onwards) is an automatic conversion between primitive types and wrapper classes.

57. Any exception that extends from *RuntimeException* is considered an unchecked exception. Unchecked exceptions need not be caught by catch block. The compiler does not forces the control to handle unchecked exceptions. An exception that the compiler forces to coder to handle are known as checked exceptions. Typically, it is achieved using a try/catch block. All checked exceptions are inherited from *java.lang.Exception* class, but do not extend the *java.lang.RuntimeException* class.

58. In Java, objects and primitive types are passed by value. For a primitive type, the value is whatever is assigned before it was created. For an object, the value is the actual object reference. Every object references in the JVM are 32-bit integers(system dependent) which JVM maps to memory addresses.

59. Heap is a part of memory which is used while executing an program. It is used to store data dynamically created data at run-time. New instances(objects) are always stored in the heap.

60. An object is qualified for garbage collection when no live thread can access it. If all the reference variables that refers to the object are set to *null*, the object becomes qualified for garbage collection. Objects created locally in a method are eligible for garbage collection when the method returns, unless they are exported out of the method (that is, returned or thrown as an exception). Objects that refer to each other can still be eligible for garbage collection.

61. Uniform Resource Locator (URL) is a standard for writing a textual reference to data in the WWW. A URL looks like *protocol://host/info*, where *protocol* specifies a protocol like HTTP or FTP to be used to fetch the object. The *host* specifies the internet name of the host on which to find and *info* is a string passed to the protocol handler on the remote host.

62. The *final* keyword is used to prevent changes of content from others. Instances of a final class can be created. The *final* is similar to constant in C/C++ and *final* methods cannot be overridden. Final class cannot be inherited.

63. Free pool of memory or method area memory is used for *String str = "hello";* and Heap memory is for *String str2 = new String("hello");*. In the second case, if the content is same then points to same string. If *String* value is modified, then it creates a new *String* every time.

64. Static variables are declared in classes or methods with *static* modifier. Only one copy is stored in *static* memory associated to a class (class variables). It is created/initialized during class loading in memory.

65. If *abstract* method is *private*, it cannot be overridden in the subclass. So declaring a method as *abstract* and *private* does not make any sense.

66. Space for objects created with the *new* operator is allocated from the heap. Local variables or method arguments of primitive types are created on the stack. Objects created in the heap have a longer lifetime. Objects remain in the heap as long as the objects contain instance variables of primitive types. However, these primitive variables are kept on the heap as well.

67. An object can be finalized only once. An object has exactly one lock and is independent of its class. A thread can reacquire the lock on the same object and it can have locks on multiple objects at the same time.

68. The *final* variable can be assigned value only once.

69. If single method performs different task, it is known as polymorphism. There are two types of polymorphism. Where one type is (i)Compile time polymorphism and another type is (ii) run time polymorphism.

70. Control statements: *if-else, switch, while, do-while, for, break* and *continue*.

71. The keyword *new* creates a new instance of the specific class and allocates the necessary memory from the heap. Then, it calls the constructor method of the object and returns a reference to the new object created.

72. *BufferedReaders* are used to read input from a file or the keyboard.

73. An array reference can be declared with one of the following equivalent syntaxes : *int[] a;* or *int a[];*. An array is object and it is stored in the heap. Array declaration allocates memory space for a reference and its default value is *null*.

74. A package is a logical set of class definitions. These classes are of numerous files, where all files are stored in the same directory. Each package defines a new scope (i.e., it puts bounds to visibility of names). It is then possible to use unchanged class names in different package with no name conflicts.

75. A package is identified by a name with a hierarchic structure (fully qualified name), e.g. *java.lang.String*.

76. Wrapper classes are defined in *java.lang* package. Primitive types and its respective wrapper class are given in table below,

Primitive Type	Wrapper Class
boolean	Boolean
char	Character
byte	Byte
short	Short
int	Integer
long	Long
float	Float
double	Double
void	Void

77. Application Programmer Interface (API) is used by application to accesses the facilities of some object.

78. Remote Procedure Call (RPC) is a process of method invocation in some remote host by sending instruction over the network.

79. The *IOException* exception is in *java.io* package and used to handle input/output errors.

80. The *implements* keyword is used when a class needs to use an interface.

81. A *HashSet* is an unordered *Set*. It uses the *hashcode* of the object being inserted. This class is recommended when a collection with no duplicates and order is not required.

82. GUI components like *textbox, label, button, images* can be included in a Java frame.

83. JAVADOC comments starts with the tag /**, following intermediate lines begin with character * and finally the multiline comments are terminated by the tag */. JAVADOC comments are official documentation of your code.

84. To reserve a space in memory as immutable, *final* keyword should be used. e.g. *final int a = 1000;*

85. The !(negation) operator can be prefixed any boolean variable or expression. It results in the logical value of the variable or expression.

86. Concatenation is the process by which two or more strings are joined together.

87. Marker interfaces do not declare any needed methods, but signify their compatibility with certain operations, e.g. *java.io.Serializable* interface and *Cloneable* interface. These do not include any methods, but classes must implement this interface in order to be serialized and de-serialized.

88. *java.lang* package is imported by default into Java programs.

89. The *try-catch* block contains the business code to execute, if the exception in the *try* statement is thrown during the code execution, then it runs the code in the catch block. While *try-catch-finally* works the same way as *try-catch* block with the addition of *finally* block which will execute whether an error occurs or not.

90. Rules of naming variables: (i) No spaces or symbols in variable names (ii) Variable names cannot start with numbers, (iii) Variable names can only contain letters, numbers and underscore (_) symbol.

91. The *switch* statements are used to test a variable for N different values.

92. An instance of a class which is also an instance of its superclass is called Polymorphism.

93. Four principle concepts of object oriented design and programming are, (i) Abstraction, (ii) Polymorphism, (iii) Inheritance and (iv) Encapsulation.

94. Binding is the process of linking a procedure call to the code that is to be executed in response to a call. Dynamic binding/late binding is the process of associating code with a given procedure call during the call at run-time (due to polymorphism and inheritance).

95. Rules of overloading,
    a. A method can be overloaded in the same class or in a subclass.
    b. Overloaded methods can declare new or broader checked exceptions.
    c. Overloaded methods must change the argument list.
    d. Overloaded methods can change the return type.
    e. Overloaded methods can change the access modifier.

96. The *main* method cannot override, because it is a *static* method. Further, *static* method cannot be overridden in the Java(before Java-7).

97. Rules to use *interface* are as follows,
    a. *Interface* variables must be *static*.
    b. Interfaces cannot be instantiated.
    c. Interfaces may have member variables, but these are implicitly *static*, *public* and *final*.
    d. *Interface* cannot be defined as *final*.
    e. An *interface* can extend other interfaces.
    f. Only *public* and *abstract* modifiers are allowed for methods in interfaces.

98. Properties of *Set* interface are,
    a. The *Set* interface provides methods for accessing the elements of a finite mathematical set.
    b. *Sets* interface do not allow duplicate elements.
    c. Does not contain any methods, that are not inherited from *Collection*.
    d. Two *Set* objects are equal if they contain the same elements.
    e. Implementation of *Set* interface are *HashSet, TreeSet, LinkedHashSet* and *EnumSet*.

99. A *Map* is an object that stores associations between keys and values pairs. Given a key, you can find its respective value. Where, both keys and values are objects. However, keys must be unique, but the values may be duplicated. Maps can accept *null* key and *null* values.

100. A *TreeMap* implements the *SortedMap* interface, which extends *Map* interface. In a *TreeMap*, the data will be ordered in ascending order based on keys or by the comparator provided at formation time. *TreeMap* uses Red-Black tree data structure.

101. The *Comparable* interface is used to order (sort) arrays of objects and collections using the *java.utils.Arrays.sort()* and *Collections.sort()* methods respectively. The objects of the class implementing the *Comparable* interface can be sorted.

102. Some uses and properties of *Iterator* are as follows,
    a. Iterators allows to process each element of a *Collection*. *Iterator* is an interface implemented in a special way for every *Collection*.
    b. The *Iterator* interface is used to traverse through the elements of a *Collection*.
    c. Iterators are a generic way to go through all the elements of a *Collection* no matter how it is organized.
    d. *Iterator* also has a method *remove()* which can be used to remove the current element in the iteration.
    e. An iterator at the start of the collection is required to traverse through the collection. Then, using a loop, iterate as long as *hasNext()* returns true. Within the loop, obtain the next element by calling *next()*.

103. *List* interface provides ordered collections of objects. Lists may contain duplicate elements.

Index

KEY FEATURES OF THE BOOK...

=> Provides Java-7/8 aptitude questions to improve your programming skills.
=> Lists differences between the concepts of Java-7/8.
=> Highlights Frequently Asked Questions(FAQs).
=> Exercises your aptitude skills.
=> Handbook for professionals.